HEINEMANN MATHEMATICS 8

Textbook

These are the different types of pages and symbols used in this book:

This book is in four Parts. Each Part contains a number of sections relating to different areas of mathematics.

These pages develop mathematical skills, concepts and facts in a wide variety of realistic contexts.

Extended contexts require the use of skills from several different areas of mathematics in a section of work based on a single theme.

Detours provide self-contained activities which often require an exploratory, investigative approach drawing on problem-solving skills.

This symbol shows when you need to use a page from the accompanying workbook.

This is a reminder of key information essential for the work of the page.

Challenges are more-demanding activities designed to stimulate further thought and discussion.

Investigations enhance the work of the page by providing additional opportunities to develop and use problem-solving skills.

Contents

The Borders Bank

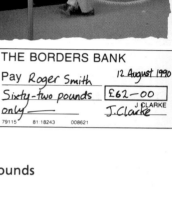

Jean is a teller in the Borders Bank.
When customers write cheques she makes
sure that they write the same amount in
words and in figures.

1 Complete the cheques on **Workbook page 2.**

2 Jean only has £100 notes, £10 notes and £1 coins.
She gives customers as few notes and coins as possible.
She gave Roger six £10 notes and two £1 coins.
Which notes and coins should she give these customers?
(a) Sheila Gray, £84   **(b)** Celie York, £230
(c) John Walker, £357 **(d)** Ali Amir, £1600
(e) Mark Smith, two thousand eight hundred and ninety pounds
(f) Ann Black, five hundred and seven pounds.

THE BORDERS BANK

Pay *Roger Smith*   *12 August 1990*

Sixty-two pounds   £62—00

only   *J.Clarke*
J CLARKE

79115   81 18243   008621

3 During one week Jean handled 342 cheques.
342 lies between 340 and 350.

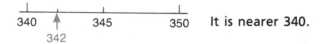

340   345   350   It is nearer 340.
342

Jean handled 340 cheques rounded **to the nearest ten.**

Teller	Number of cheques
Jean	342
Salim	257
Vicky	84
Peter	105

(a) Round **to the nearest ten** the number of cheques
handled by each of the other tellers.
(b) **Exactly** how many cheques were handled by the tellers altogether?
Round this total **to the nearest ten**.

4 During this week Jean served 768 customers.
768 lies between 700 and 800.

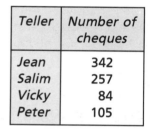

700   750   800   It is nearer 800.
768

Jean served 800 customers rounded **to the nearest hundred**.

(a) Round **to the nearest hundred** the
number of customers served by each
of the other tellers.
(b) Calculate exactly the total number of
customers served by the tellers.
Round this total **to the nearest
hundred**.

	Jean	Salim	Vicky	Peter
Number of customers	768	637	1195	850

5 Jean had £3821 in cash at the end of one day.
She had **£4000** rounded **to the nearest thousand**.
(a) Round **to the nearest thousand** each of the other
amounts.
(b) Exactly how much did the tellers have altogether?
Round this amount **to the nearest thousand**.

	Amount of cash
Jean	£3821
Salim	£2417
Vicky	£4635
Peter	£3570

6 Do Workbook page 2, question 2.

Jill sells ice creams. She often needs to multiply prices.

1 Find:
- **(a)** 2×83
- **(b)** 65 times 7
- **(c)** 25×8
- **(d)** 520 multiplied by 4
- **(e)** 6 multiplied by 275
- **(f)** 5 lots of 170
- **(g)** the product of 9 and 308

Remember

To multiply by **10**, move each digit **one** place to the left.   23×10 = 230

To multiply by **100**, move each digit **two** places to the left.   23×100 = 2300

To multiply by **1000**, move each digit **three** places to the left.   23×1000=23 000

2 Find mentally:
- **(a)** 13×10
- **(b)** 100×17
- **(c)** 1000×79
- **(d)** 910×10
- **(e)** 123×100
- **(f)** 20×1000
- **(g)** 100×720
- **(h)** 1000×103

Jill buys nougat wafers in boxes of 300. She has 24 boxes.
How many nougat wafers does she have?
She has 24×300 nougat wafers.

or 24×100 → 2400 then 2400×3 → 7200
24×3 → 72 then 72×100 → 7200 so **24×300 → 7200**

NOUGAT WAFERS 300

There are **7200** nougat wafers in 24 boxes.

To multiply by 20,   multiply by 10, then by 2   **or** multiply by 2, then by 10.

To multiply by 6000, multiply by 1000, then by 6 **or** multiply by 6, then by 1000.

3 How many cones are there in 144 packs of 20?

4 How many plain wafers are there in 12 boxes of 6000?

5 Ice lollies come in packs of 15. How many are there in
- **(a)** 400 packs
- **(b)** 600 packs
- **(c)** 3000 packs
- **(d)** 5000 packs?

6 Find mentally:
- **(a)** 2×30
- **(b)** 20×30
- **(c)** 200×30
- **(d)** 200×300
- **(e)** 30×50
- **(f)** 30×500
- **(g)** 300×500
- **(h)** 300×5000

24 is about 20   *o 36 is about 40*

Approximately how many flakes are there in a value box?

There are 24×36 flakes in a value box.

You can find an approximate answer to 24×36 like this:

FLAKE FLAKES 24 PACKS OF 36 VALUE BOX

So the answer is **about 20×40 → 800**.
There are about **800** flakes in a value box.

7 Approximately how many flakes are there in a carton which holds
- **(a)** 48 packs
- **(b)** 72 packs
- **(c)** 104 packs
- **(d)** 75 packs?

8 Estimate the cost of
- **(a)** 72 choc ices at 18p each
- **(b)** 36 ice cream tubs at 27p each
- **(c)** 66 cartons of juice at 33p each
- **(d)** 288 litres of ice cream at 42p per litre.

Company cars

*How far can I travel on a full tank of **diesel**?*

The tank holds 56 litres. The car averages 17 km per litre. So the distance is 17 × 56 km.

1 Bill Gibson is collecting his new company car from the garage.
How many kilometres can he travel on a full tank of diesel fuel?

2 Bill's old company car had a **petrol** tank which held 72 litres.
The old car averaged 13 kilometres per litre. How far could
he travel in this car on a full tank of petrol?

3 Bill Gibson's company has been using 4 other makes of car.

Calculate how far each car can travel on a full tank of petrol.

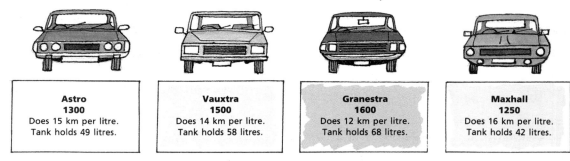

| **Astro** **1300** Does 15 km per litre. Tank holds 49 litres. | **Vauxtra** **1500** Does 14 km per litre. Tank holds 58 litres. | **Granestra** **1600** Does 12 km per litre. Tank holds 68 litres. | **Maxhall** **1250** Does 16 km per litre. Tank holds 42 litres. |

4 The company replaced its fleet of 25 old cars with new models, like Bill's.
(a) Each new car cost £9640. What was the total cost of the 25 new cars?
(b) Each old car was sold for £3200. How much did the company receive?
(c) How much did it cost the company to replace its fleet of cars?

5 Bill drives an average of 1850 kilometres per month. He expects to get his next new
car in 2 years time. How far should he have travelled by then?

In September Bill travelled 2030 km.

1200 × 18p → 21 600p = £216·00
830 × 15p → 12 450p = £124·50
                             £340·50

His petrol expenses were **£340·50**

MAZE COMPANY   Memo

To ___Company car holders___
From ___Financial director___
Petrol expenses are paid each month at
these rates; 18p per km for the first
1200 km, 15p per km after that.

6 How much were his petrol expenses in
(a) August, 1470 km **(b)** July, 1974 km **(c)** June, 2216 km?

7 For his new diesel car Bill is paid monthly expenses of 14p per km for the first 800 km
12p per km for the next 1000 km
10p per km after that.

Copy and complete the table below.

Distance in km	1600	1800	2000	2200
Expenses in £				

1 George works at Rynan's. He has to do calculations like these.
Help him find:

  (a) $48 \div 3$ **(b)** $207 \div 9$ **(c)** $7\overline{)973}$ **(d)** 1818 divided by 6   **(e)** $\dfrac{768}{8}$

To divide by **10**, move each digit **one** place to the right.	$18\,000 \div 10 \quad = 1800$
To divide by **100**, move each digit **two** places to the right.	$18\,000 \div 100 \quad = \quad 180$
To divide by **1000**, move each digit **three** places to the right.	$18\,000 \div 1000 = \quad 18$

Remember

2 Find mentally:

  (a) $240 \div 10$ **(b)** $3000 \div 100$ **(c)** $14\,000 \div 1000$ **(d)** $\dfrac{600}{10}$ **(e)** $1000\overline{)173\,000}$

A customer asks George for 8000 envelopes.
How many boxes does George need?

He needs $8000 \div 500$ boxes.

or $\begin{array}{l} 8000 \div 100 \rightarrow 80 \quad \text{then} \quad 80 \div 5 \rightarrow 16 \\ 8000 \div 5 \rightarrow 1600 \text{ then } 1600 \div 100 \rightarrow 16 \end{array}$ so **$8000 \div 500 \rightarrow 16$**

George needs **16** boxes.

To divide by **50**,   divide by 10 and then by 6   **or** divide by 6 and then by 10.

To divide by **3000**, divide by 1000 and then by 3 **or** divide by 3 and then by 1000.

3 A box holds 500 sheets of paper. How many boxes are needed for

  (a) 3000 sheets   **(b)** 10 000 sheets   **(c)** 24 000 sheets?

4 Rynan's sells folders in packets of 40. How many packets can George make up from

  (a) 400 folders   **(b)** 2000 folders   **(c)** 12 000 folders?

5 A carton holds 5000 paper clips. How many cartons does George need for

  (a) 15 000 paper clips   **(b)** 120 000 paper clips   **(c)** 250 000 paper clips?

6 Labels cost £8 for 200. How much does one label cost in pence?

Approximately how many cartons of pens will George sell?

An approximate answer can be found like this:

580 is about 600   36 is about 40

So the answer is **about $600 \div 40 \rightarrow 15$**

He will sell about **15** cartons.

580 is almost 600

36 is about 40

580 pens please

7 George packs sets of coloured pencils in boxes of different sizes. **Approximately**
how many boxes are needed for 630 sets when each box holds

  (a) 18 sets   **(b)** 36 sets   **(c)** 48 sets   **(d)** 96 sets?

Sharon is the warden at the Achindall Youth Hostel.
She has ordered some bedding.

SLEEPEEZIE BEDDING COMPANY
Order Form
Please supply Achindall Youth Hostel, Inverdale.

Quantity	Item	Cost
32	Beds at £69 each	
32	Mattresses at £41 each	
39	Duvets at £28 each	
64	Pillows at £13 per pair	
	Sleeping bags at £9 each	£432

1 Find the **approximate** cost of

   (a) the beds   (b) the mattresses   (c) the duvets.

2 How many sleeping bags did she order?

3 **Use a calculator.** Copy and complete the order form.
   Find the **total** cost.

4 Sharon hoped to collect enough money in hostel fees to pay
   for the bedding in one year. On average how much should
   she collect each week?

5 She collected an average of £36 per day from hostelers.
   How much was this   (a) per week   (b) per year?

6 Was this enough to pay both the Sleepeezie Bedding
   Company *and* Sharon's salary of £7020 per year? Explain.

7 How much does Sharon earn each week?

Sharon bought cream rice and bean stew
from the Cash and Carry.

8 (a) What was the cost in pence of
      one tin of cream rice?

   (b) She sold cream rice at 55p per tin.
      What was her profit if she sold all
      the cream rice?

9 She sold the bean stew at 65p per tin. What
   was her profit if she sold all the bean stew?

10 How much profit did she make altogether
   on the cream rice and the bean stew?

Challenge

11 (a) When Sharon had sold these 10 tins her
      profit was 82p. How many of each tin had she sold?

   (b) When she had sold exactly 20 tins her profit was
      £1·56. How many of each tin had she sold?

   (c) How many **full boxes** of each would she have to
      sell to make a profit of £13·08?

Ask your teacher what to do next.

A flowchart lists instructions.
You have to follow them in order.

Every flowchart has
- a title
- (Start) and (Stop) boxes
- Instruction boxes
- arrows between boxes

1 Do Workbook page 3.

2 (a) Design a flowchart which always gives the answer 6.
Use these instructions.

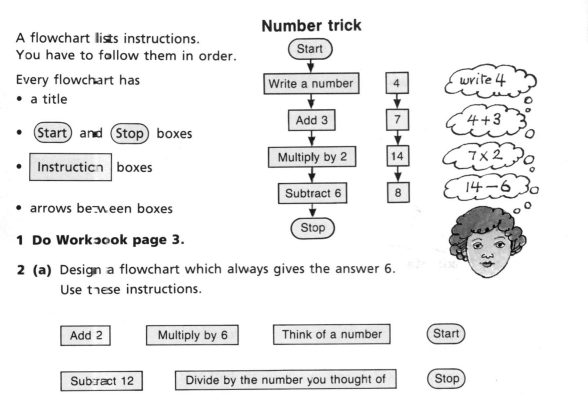

Number trick

(b) Check your flowchart works using at least 3 starting numbers.

3 (a) Read this flowchart. Check that the correct path has been followed for each of the starting numbers 3 and 10.

Number puzzle

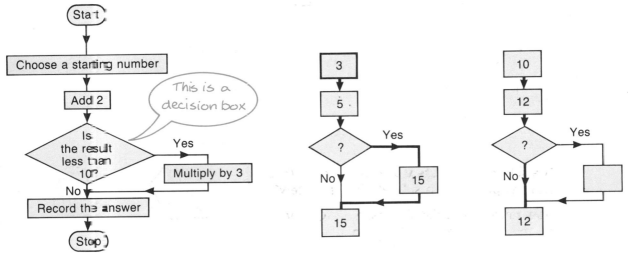

(b) Copy and complete the table.

Starting number	3	10	7	4	12	21	8
Answer	15						

Ask your teacher what to do next.

1 Make a collection of pictures which show examples of line symmetry.

2 **Do Workbook page 1.**

3 Which of these flags have
  (a) a vertical axis of symmetry
  (b) a horizontal axis of symmetry
  (c) both a vertical axis and a
      horizontal axis of symmetry
  (d) no axes of symmetry?

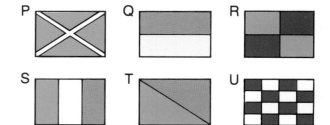

4 Trace each flag. Rotate each tracing on top of the flag.
  How often does each tracing match the flag in one full turn?
  Record your results like this: **P matches 2 times in one full turn.**

5 Trace each of these designs. Find out how many times each
  tracing matches its design in one full turn.

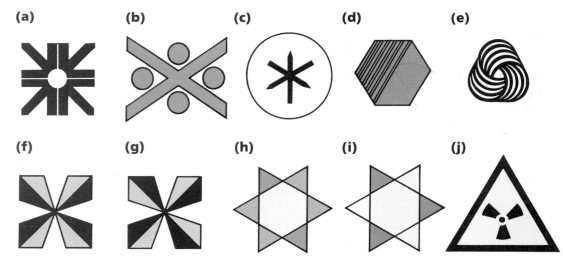

6 How many axes of symmetry has each design?

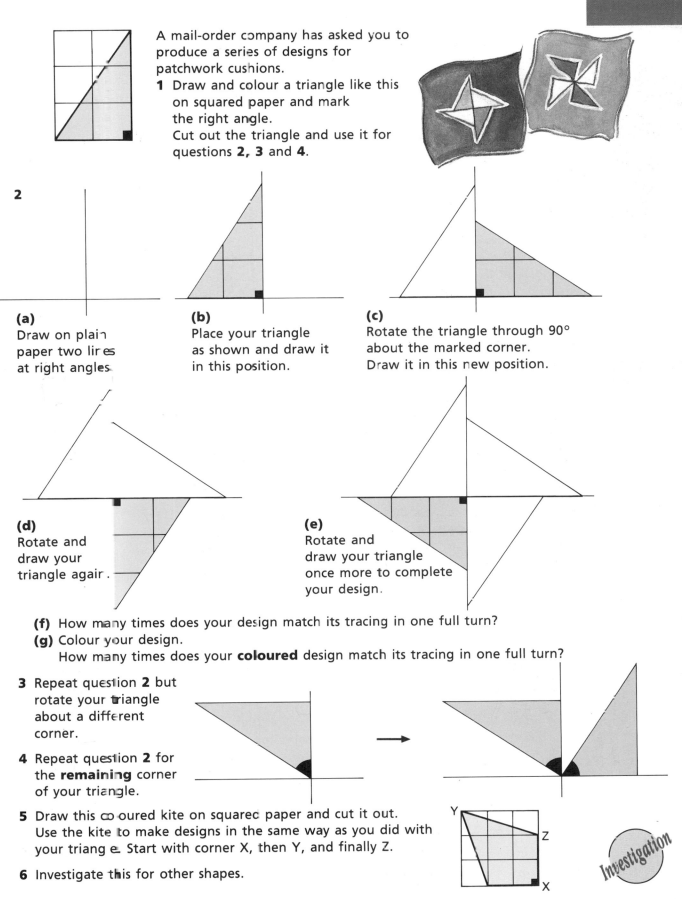

A mail-order company has asked you to
produce a series of designs for
patchwork cushions.

1 Draw and colour a triangle like this
on squared paper and mark
the right angle.
Cut out the triangle and use it for
questions **2, 3** and **4**.

2

(a)
Draw on plain
paper two lines
at right angles.

(b)
Place your triangle
as shown and draw it
in this position.

(c)
Rotate the triangle through 90°
about the marked corner.
Draw it in this new position.

(d)
Rotate and
draw your
triangle again.

(e)
Rotate and
draw your triangle
once more to complete
your design.

(f) How many times does your design match its tracing in one full turn?

(g) Colour your design.
How many times does your **coloured** design match its tracing in one full turn?

3 Repeat question **2** but
rotate your triangle
about a different
corner.

4 Repeat question **2** for
the **remaining** corner
of your triangle.

5 Draw this coloured kite on squared paper and cut it out.
Use the kite to make designs in the same way as you did with
your triangle. Start with corner X, then Y, and finally Z.

6 Investigate this for other shapes.

Investigation

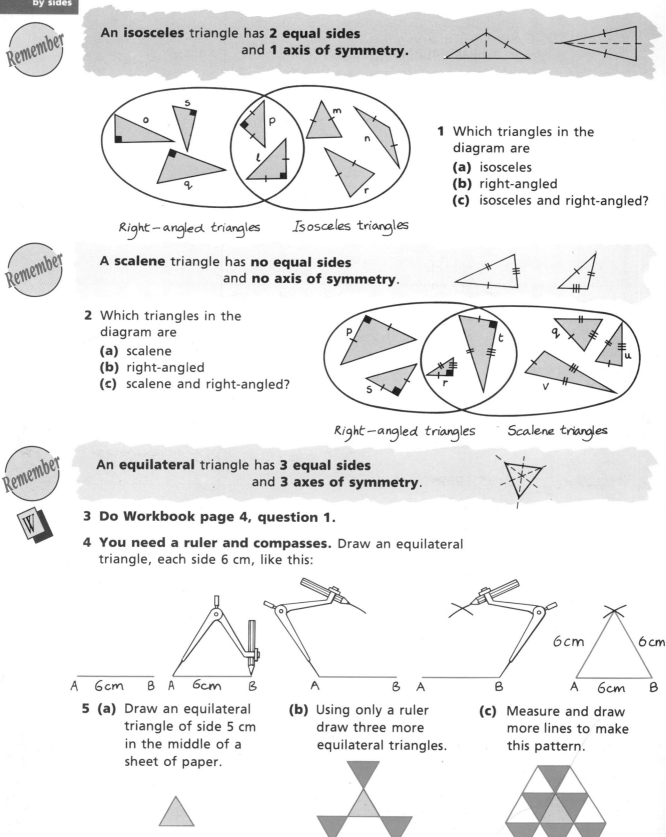

Remember

An **isosceles** triangle has **2 equal sides** and **1 axis of symmetry**.

Right–angled triangles   Isosceles triangles

1 Which triangles in the diagram are
  (a) isosceles
  (b) right-angled
  (c) isosceles and right-angled?

Remember

A **scalene** triangle has **no equal sides** and **no axis of symmetry**.

2 Which triangles in the diagram are
  (a) scalene
  (b) right-angled
  (c) scalene and right-angled?

Right–angled triangles   Scalene triangles

Remember

An **equilateral** triangle has **3 equal sides** and **3 axes of symmetry**.

3 Do Workbook page 4, question 1.

4 You need a ruler and compasses. Draw an equilateral triangle, each side 6 cm, like this:

A 6cm B A 6cm B   A   B A   B   6cm ⟋ ⟍ 6cm
                                                                A 6cm B

5 (a) Draw an equilateral triangle of side 5 cm in the middle of a sheet of paper.

(b) Using only a ruler draw three more equilateral triangles.

(c) Measure and draw more lines to make this pattern.

(d) Draw the axes of symmetry on your pattern.

These are **obtuse-angled** triangles.
They each have **one obtuse angle** and **two acute angles.**

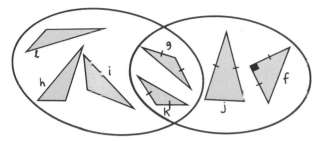

Obtuse-angled triangles   Isosceles triangles

1 Which triangles in the
diagram are
   (a) obtuse-angled
   (b) isosceles
   (c) obtuse-angled and isosceles?

2 These are **acute-angled** triangles
What kind of angle is **every** angle
in each triangle?

3 Which triangles in the
diagram are
   (a) acute-angled
   (b) scalene
   (c) acute-angled and scalene?

4 Do Workbook page 4, question 2.

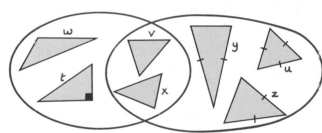

Scalene triangles   Acute-angled triangles

5 You need **½ cm squared paper.**

   (a) Plot the following sets of points on separate diagrams.
   Join the points to make triangles.

   L → (1,1), (6,2), (4,3)   M → (1,1), (1,3), (8,2)
   N → (8,2), (5,5), (2,2)   O → (2,0), (5,6), (6,0)
   P → (2,7), (4,4), (2,1)   Q → (1,3), (3,5), (7,1)
   R → (1,1), (3,4), (8,6)   S → (0,0), (5,0), (0,5)

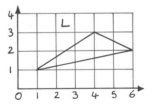

   (b) Copy the table. Enter the letters of
   the triangles L to S in your table.

	Acute-angled	Right-angled	Obtuse-angled
Isosceles			
Scalene			L

**6 You need a 9-pin nailboard, elastic bands, and the grids
on Workbook page 4, question 3.**

The triangle on the nailboard is an obtuse-angled scalene
triangle. Make as many **different** triangles as possible on a
9-pin nailboard. Each time you make a different triangle draw
it in the workbook and name it.

Investigation

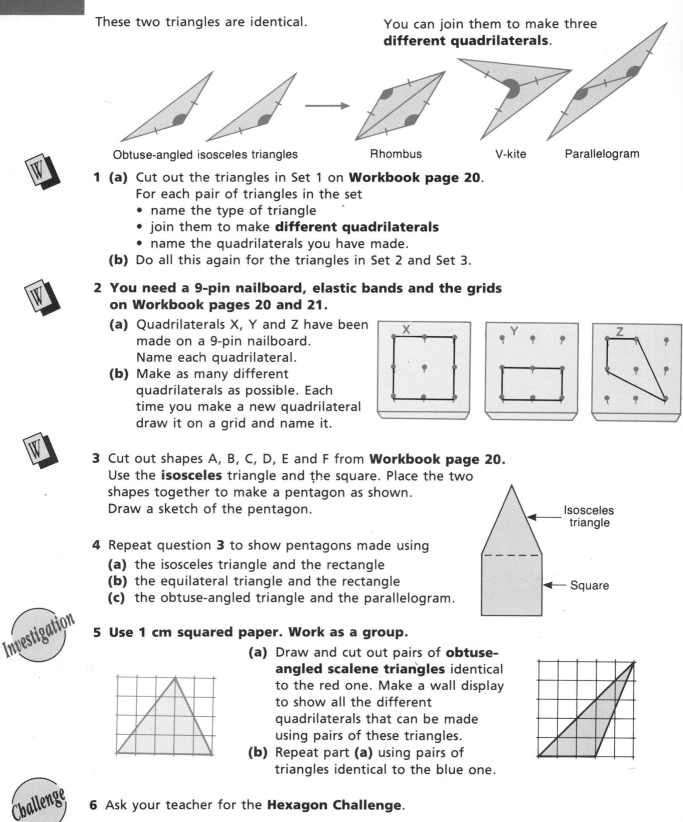

These two triangles are identical.

You can join them to make three **different quadrilaterals**.

Obtuse-angled isosceles triangles · Rhombus · V-kite · Parallelogram

1 (a) Cut out the triangles in Set 1 on **Workbook page 20**.
For each pair of triangles in the set
- name the type of triangle
- join them to make **different quadrilaterals**
- name the quadrilaterals you have made.

(b) Do all this again for the triangles in Set 2 and Set 3.

**2 You need a 9-pin nailboard, elastic bands and the grids
on Workbook pages 20 and 21.**

(a) Quadrilaterals X, Y and Z have been
made on a 9-pin nailboard.
Name each quadrilateral.

(b) Make as many different
quadrilaterals as possible. Each
time you make a new quadrilateral
draw it on a grid and name it.

3 Cut out shapes A, B, C, D, E and F from **Workbook page 20**.
Use the **isosceles** triangle and the square. Place the two
shapes together to make a pentagon as shown.
Draw a sketch of the pentagon.

Isosceles
triangle

Square

4 Repeat question **3** to show pentagons made using
(a) the isosceles triangle and the rectangle
(b) the equilateral triangle and the rectangle
(c) the obtuse-angled triangle and the parallelogram.

Investigation

5 Use 1 cm squared paper. Work as a group.

(a) Draw and cut out pairs of **obtuse-
angled scalene triangles** identical
to the red one. Make a wall display
to show all the different
quadrilaterals that can be made
using pairs of these triangles.

(b) Repeat part **(a)** using pairs of
triangles identical to the blue one.

Challenge

6 Ask your teacher for the **Hexagon Challenge**.

Ask your teacher what to do next.

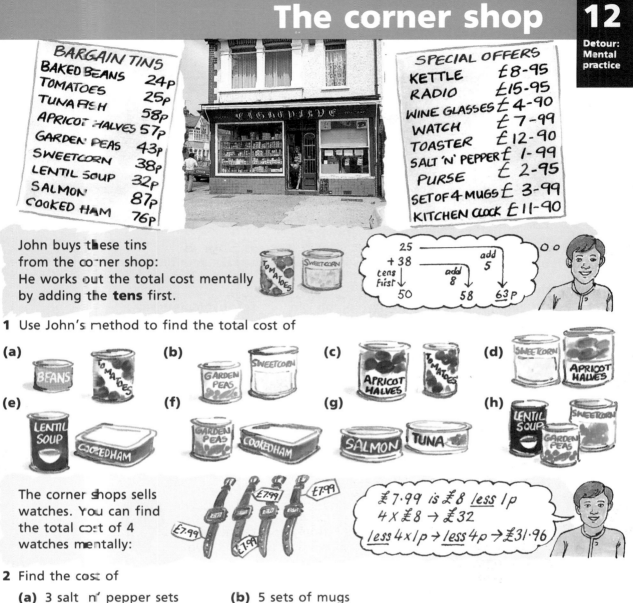

BARGAIN TINS
BAKED BEANS 24p
TOMATOES 25p
TUNA FISH 58p
APRICOT HALVES 57p
GARDEN PEAS 43p
SWEETCORN 38p
LENTIL SOUP 32p
SALMON 87p
COOKED HAM 76p

SPECIAL OFFERS
KETTLE £8-95
RADIO £15-95
WINE GLASSES £4-90
WATCH £7-99
TOASTER £12-90
SALT 'N' PEPPER £1-99
PURSE £2-95
SET OF 4 MUGS £3-99
KITCHEN CLOCK £11-90

John buys these tins
from the corner shop:
He works out the total cost mentally
by adding the **tens** first.

25
+ 38
tens first ↓ → 50   add 8 → 58   add 5 → 63p

1 Use John's method to find the total cost of

(a) BEANS TOMATOES

(b) GARDEN PEAS SWEETCORN

(c) APRICOT HALVES TOMATOES

(d) SWEETCORN APRICOT HALVES

(e) LENTIL SOUP COOKED HAM

(f) GARDEN PEAS COOKED HAM

(g) SALMON TUNA

(h) LENTIL SOUP SWEETCORN GARDEN PEAS

The corner shops sells
watches. You can find
the total cost of 4
watches mentally:

£7.99   £7.99   £7.99   £7.99

£7.99 is £8 less 1p
4 × £8 → £32
less 4 × 1p → less 4p → £31·96

2 Find the cost of
    (a) 3 salt 'n' pepper sets   **(b)** 5 sets of mugs
    (c) 4 purses   **(d)** 5 kettles
    (e) 4 radios   **(f)** 6 sets of wine glasses
    (g) 1 watch **and** 1 set of mugs   **(h)** 1 radio **and** 1 purse
    (i) 1 kettle **and** 1 radio   **(j)** 1 toaster **and** 1 set of wine glasses.

3 Here are five sets of prices.
The shopkeeper has written them
in two different orders.
For each set, which order is easier
to add?

	Order 1	Order 2
(a)	7p + 18p + 3p	7p + 3p + 18p
(b)	26p + 8p + 2p	8p + 2p + 26p
(c)	14p + 6p + 9p	9p + 14p + 6p
(d)	40p + 53p + 60p	60p + 40p + 53p
(e)	75p + 25p + 29p	75p + 29p + 25p

4 Add these mentally. Use the easiest order each time.
    (a) 15p + 5p + 7p   **(b)** 3p + 19p + 7p   **(c)** 8p + 36p + 12p
    (d) 40p + 58p + 60p   **(e)** 18p + 17p + 12p   **(f)** 5p + 18p + 15p + 2p
    (g) 7p + 26p + 4p + 13p   **(h)** 65p + 18p + 35p   **(i)** £5 + £8·70 + £5
    (j) 16p + £3·20 + 24p   **(k)** 99p + 88p + 1p + 2p   **(l)** £4 + 72p + 28p + £1·50

Ask your teacher what to do next.

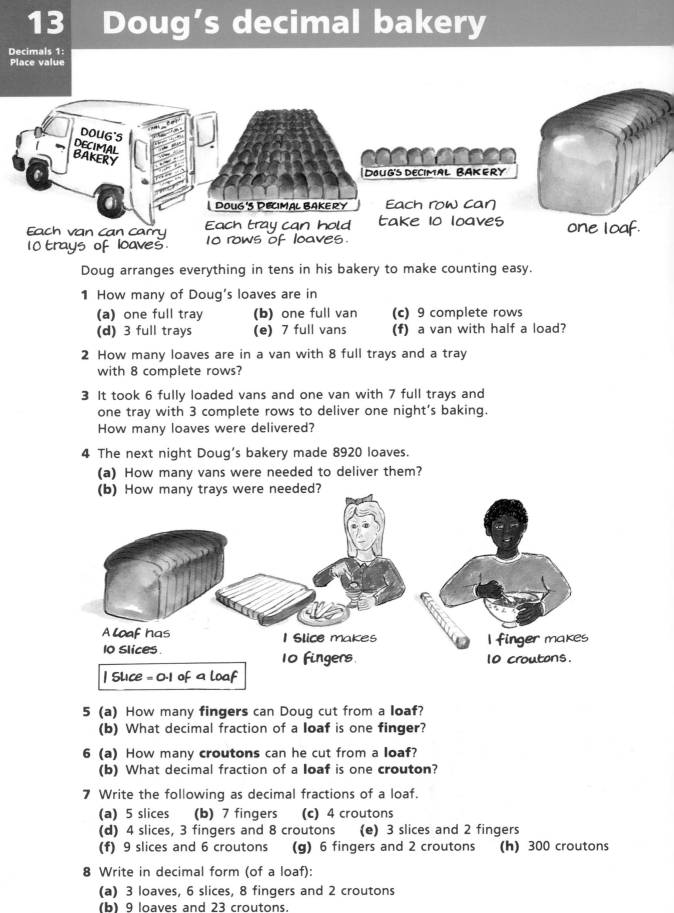

Each van can carry 10 trays of loaves.

Each tray can hold 10 rows of loaves.

Each row can take 10 loaves

one loaf.

Doug arranges everything in tens in his bakery to make counting easy.

1 How many of Doug's loaves are in

(a) one full tray   (b) one full van   (c) 9 complete rows

(d) 3 full trays   (e) 7 full vans   (f) a van with half a load?

2 How many loaves are in a van with 8 full trays and a tray with 8 complete rows?

3 It took 6 fully loaded vans and one van with 7 full trays and one tray with 3 complete rows to deliver one night's baking. How many loaves were delivered?

4 The next night Doug's bakery made 8920 loaves.

(a) How many vans were needed to deliver them?

(b) How many trays were needed?

A **loaf** has 10 **slices**.

| 1 slice = 0·1 of a loaf |

1 **slice** makes 10 **fingers**.

1 **finger** makes 10 **croutons**.

5 (a) How many **fingers** can Doug cut from a **loaf**?

(b) What decimal fraction of a **loaf** is one **finger**?

6 (a) How many **croutons** can he cut from a **loaf**?

(b) What decimal fraction of a **loaf** is one **crouton**?

7 Write the following as decimal fractions of a loaf.

(a) 5 slices   (b) 7 fingers   (c) 4 croutons

(d) 4 slices, 3 fingers and 8 croutons   (e) 3 slices and 2 fingers

(f) 9 slices and 6 croutons   (g) 6 fingers and 2 croutons   (h) 300 croutons

8 Write in decimal form (of a loaf):

(a) 3 loaves, 6 slices, 8 fingers and 2 croutons

(b) 9 loaves and 23 croutons.

9 Do Workbook page 5.

The Dudley Dolphins swimming club sells these items.

 T-Shirt £5·24

 Scarf £2·70

Swimming Cap £4

Club Pen 65p

Metal Badge 75p

2 Stickers 8p

1 Find how much each of these club members spent in pounds.

   (a) Lynton bought a cap and a badge

   (b) Julie bought a T-shirt and a scarf

   (c) Ahmed bought a pen and a badge

   (d) Andy bought a T-shirt and 2 stickers

   (e) Lisa bought a cap and 2 stickers

   (f) Jackson bought a T-shirt, a badge and 2 stickers.

2 Sally bought a T-shirt, a scarf and a pen.
How much change did she get from £10?

3 Vijay wants to buy all 6 items.
How much will he save in the Special
Offer?

DUDLEY DOLPHINS
Special Offer
All 6 items only
£10·99

4 This is Heather's receipt for two items.

   (a) What two items did she buy?

   (b) Calculate her change.

   (c) What four coins was she given as change?

Total £5·89
Amount Tendered £6·00
Change £

5 Here are the Dudley Dolphins
Synchro Swim team marks. For each
swimmer the highest and lowest
marks are not counted.

   (a) Calculate the score for each swimmer.

   (b) List the swimmers in order, starting with the winner.

	Synchronised Swimming Marks						
	CAN	F	NOR	GB	SWE	USA	DEN
Rekka	5·3	6·2	5·6	5·7	5·1	6·3	6·2
Joan	5·8	5·1	6·2	6·4	5·7	6·5	5·2
Pippa	5·9	6·2	6·3	6·1	5·7	5·8	6·3
Heather	6·0	5·3	6·1	5·7	5·2	5·6	5·2

6 Here are the times, in seconds, for the eight finalists in the 50 metres freestyle.

FINALS Men's 50 metres freestyle results   (times in seconds)

Ian	Tom	Ashmid	George	Garry	Alex	Paul	Neil
26·51	27·43	26·22	26·55	27·31	28·61	26·58	27·42

   (a) List the finalists in order, starting with the winner.

   (b) What was the difference in time between the first and the last?

   (c) George beat the club record by 1·02 seconds. What was the previous record?

   (d) Which others also beat the previous club record?

   (e) What is the new club record? Who is the new record holder?

The Dudley Dolphins' minibus can travel
5·3 km on 1 litre of petrol.
It can travel 5·3 × 20 km on 20 litres of petrol
= 106 km on 20 litres of petrol.

$$5·3 × 2 = 10·6$$
$$10·6 × 10 = 106$$
So $5·3 × 20 = 106$

1 Copy and complete this table.

Number of litres	1	2	3	4	5	10	20	30	40	50
Distance in km	5·3	10·6					106			
Cost of petrol in £	0·47									

You can use your table to find how far the
minibus can travel on 22 litres of petrol.
The minibus can travel
116·6 km on 22 litres of petrol.

20 litres → 106 km
2 litres → 10·6 km
So 22 litres → 116·6 km

2 Find how far it can travel on
   (a) 13 litres **(b)** 34 litres **(c)** 29 litres of petrol.

3 Find the **cost** of
   (a) 24 litres **(b)** 43 litres **(c)** 48 litres of petrol.

4 The Dolphins will travel a total of 128 km on the outing.
   (a) Would 25 litres of petrol be enough? Explain.
   (b) Would £10 worth of petrol be enough? Explain.

5 Four members plan to take photographs of the outing.
   How much will they save altogether by sharing a pack
   of 4 films?

6 The Dolphins buy 30 cans of cola at 23p per can.
   (a) Find the total cost of the cola.
   (b) Find the total weight if each can weighs 0·35 kg.

6·4 cm

7 They put the 30 cans in a box as shown.
   Each can has a **diameter** of 6·4 cm.
   Find the inside length and breadth
   of the box.

The Dolphins went to a diving competition.

1 Use the table to find who tried
  (a) the most difficult dive **(b)** the easiest dive.

Dive	Mary			Tania			Pam		
	Mark	Difficulty	Score	Mark	Difficulty	Score	Mark	Difficulty	Score
First	26	1·7	44·2	31	1·5		26	1·7	
Second	22	2·1		28	1·6		24	1·9	
Third	24	2·0		29	1·4		23	2·4	
Fourth	27	1·9		27	1·6		26	1·8	

dive score = mark × difficulty

You can calculate the score for Mary's first dive like this:

Enter **26.** Press **×** **1** **.** **7** **=** to give **44.2**

2 (a) Calculate Mary's score for each of her dives.
  (b) Find her total score after two dives.
  (c) Find her total score after four dives.

3 Repeat question **2** for Tania and Pam.

4 Who was in the lead after

  (a) two dives **(b)** four dives?

5 There is a lift from the spectators'
  gallery.
  The members split into two groups of six.
  Is each group within the weight limit
  for the lift? Explain.

LIFT

GROUP A   GROUP B

Weight
Limit
350kg

average weight of
each person = 57·3 kg

average weight of
each person = 63·6 kg

average
weight of
each person
= 50·9 kg

6 On the way home they stopped for supper.
  The total cost of 13 suppers was £24·55.
  How many people had fish and how many had chicken?

SUPPERS
Fish £1·85
chicken £1·95

Number of persons
4   Total £59

Sally and her three friends had a meal at Roberta's. The bill came to £59.

Cost per person = £59 ÷ 4
= £14·75

14·75
4)59·00

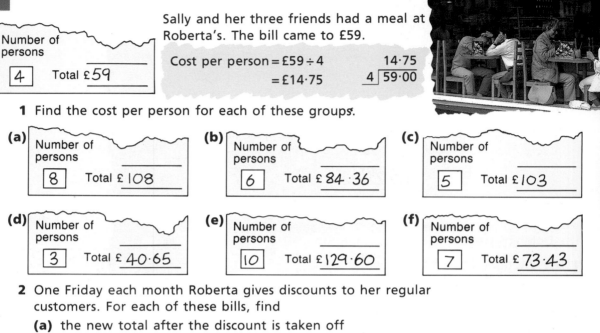

1 Find the cost per person for each of these groups.

(a) Number of persons
8   Total £108

(b) Number of persons
6   Total £84·36

(c) Number of persons
5   Total £103

(d) Number of persons
3   Total £40·65

(e) Number of persons
10   Total £129·60

(f) Number of persons
7   Total £73·43

2 One Friday each month Roberta gives discounts to her regular customers. For each of these bills, find

(a) the new total after the discount is taken off
(b) the cost per person.

 Number of persons ¼ OFF
10   Total £118·80

 Number of persons ⅕ OFF
9   Total £112·95

 Number of persons 1/10 OFF
6   Total £75

3 Roberta kept a record of the total weight of fish used by the restaurant during July. Copy and complete the table to show the average weight used **per day** for each period.

Dates	Number of days	Total weight of fish	Average weight per day
3rd to 6th July	4	74·8 kg	
7th to 16th July		206 kg	
17th to 24th July		143·2 kg	

4 Roberta wants to put in some extra tables.
The restaurant is 30 m wide. Each table is 1·5 m wide.
When 4 tables are equally spaced across the restaurant, the 5 spaces measure 30 − 6 = 24 m.
Each space is 24 ÷ 5 = 4·8 m.

30 m

1·5 m 1·5 m 1·5 m 1·5 m

(a) Find the width of each space for these numbers of tables.

Tables	4	5	6	8	9
Width of space	4·8 m				

(b) Roberta is superstitious and will not have 7 tables in a row. She must leave spaces of more than 180 cm. How many tables would **you** put in a row? Explain your answer.

You need a calculator.

At Roberta's, the waiters share the tips equally at the end of each month.
In July 7 waiters shared £146·86 of tips.

Enter `146.86`   Press `÷` `7` `=` to give `20.98`

Each waiter received £20·98 in tips for July.

1 Find the share of tips for each waiter for these months.

Month	August	September	October	November	December
Total amount of tips	£119·28	£116·10	£139·04	£86	£218·70
Number of waiters	7	6	8	8	9

2 Roberta's is open for 50 weeks of the year.

(a) Find the average takings **per week**
for each of these two years.

(b) The restaurant is open 6 days per
week. Last year it used:

1656 m sausages
5328 kg steak
4959 litres of wine

Calculate the average amount of each used **per day**.

This year £237 036

Last year £228 420

3 The table shows the total cost of meals for weeks 1 to 5.
Find the average cost **per meal** for each of these weeks.

Week number	1	2	3	4	5
Number of meals	438	391	488	512	450
Total cost of meals	£5409·30	£4828·85	£5002	£5800·96	£4977

4 Here is Roberta's staff record for one week in July:

(a) Find the hourly rate of pay for
each waiter.

(b) Who do you think is head waiter?
Explain your answer.

5 Six of the waiters are to make up a
tug-of-war team against another restaurant.

(a) If Angelo is not in the team, find
the average weight of the other six.

(b) If Angelo is included, what team
should be chosen to get as close as
possible to the maximum average weight limit of 72·5 kg?

Staff record for waiters			
Name	Hours worked	Weekly wage	Weight in kg
Arthur	35	£228·90	64·2
Clive	40	£191·60	71·7
Angelo	26	£170·04	87·6
Gavin	19	£91·01	69·9
Miguel	32	£252·80	68·1
Selim	38	£248·52	75·0
John	40	£261·60	67·5

Ask your teacher what to do next.

You can check addition by
changing the order
2345 + 1029 = 3374
Check: 1029 + 2345 = 3374

You can check multiplication
in a similar way
29 × 94 = 2736
Check: 94 × 29 = 2736

**You need a calculator.
Check each calculation by changing
the order.**

1 Find:

(a) 238 + 5620	**(b)** 19 × 56
(c) 7·62 + 345·7	**(d)** 9·9 × 13
(e) 84 + 316 + 7240	**(f)** 309 + 20·01 + 48
(g) 27 × 12 × 36	**(h)** 1·5 × 3·9 × 62

2 In a European Cup tie 42 561 spectators watched the first
game and 25 689 saw the return match. What was the total
attendance for the two games?

3 To pay his debts Lord Poker
sold these three cars. How much
did he get from the sale?

```
'79 PORSCHE 928 blue...................... £10 850
C reg DAIMLER superb condition ............. £25 500
'86 C JAGUAR SOVEREIGN 4·2.............. £16 995
```

4 Here are a carpet fitter's
measurements for four rooms.
Calculate the area of each room.
Remember to check your answers.

	Lounge	Large bedroom	Small bedroom	Box room
Length (m)	6·50	4·25	3·35	2·80
Breadth (m)	3·45	3·70	3·10	2·65

5 This is a packing case for a piece of
machinery. It is made up of two
cuboids. Calculate the total volume and
check it.

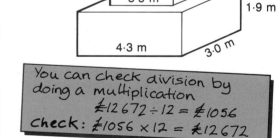

You can check subtraction by
doing an addition
£18 561 − £12 295 = £6265
Check: £6265 + £12 295 = £18 561

You can check division by
doing a multiplication
£12 672 ÷ 12 = £1056
Check: £1056 × 12 = £12 672

In the same way check your answers to the following:

6 (a) Mr and Mrs Mehta are saving to buy a TV costing £203·99.
They have saved £55. How much do they still have to save?

(b)

97 m have been used.
How much is left?

(c)

How much per packet?

(d)

How much does
one bottle cost?

(e) The total rainfall for April last year in Cardongow was 147 mm.
What was the average daily rainfall?

Ask your teacher what to do next.

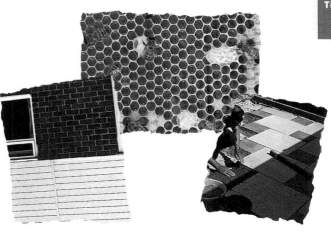

Look at the patterns in these pictures. In each pattern identical shapes (tiles) fit together without gaps or overlaps.

These patterns are called **tessellations**.

Identical shapes are called **congruent shapes**.

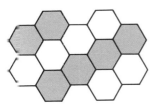

Regular hexagons tessellate.

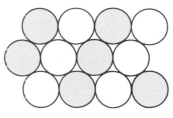

Circles do **not** tessellate.

1 Copy and extend each tessellation in all directions on square dot paper. For each draw about 12 **congruent** tiles.

(a)   **(b)**   **(c)**   **(d)**

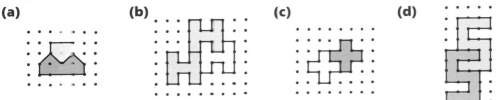

2 Copy and extend each tessellation on isometric dot paper. For each draw about 12 **congruent** tiles.

(a)   **(b)**   **(c)**

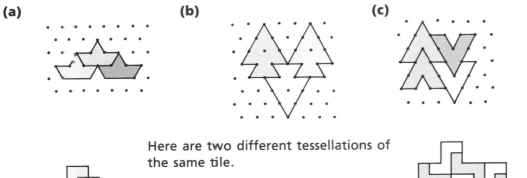

3

Here are two different tessellations of the same tile.

Experiment with dot paper to see if you can make different tessellations with each of these tiles.

Investigation

A Dutch artist, Maurits C. Escher, drew this picture. You can draw other animal pictures by altering tessellations of simple shapes.

1 Use a pencil and a rubber.

   (a) Draw 12 congruent squares
        on square dot paper as shown.

   (b) Choose one square and change its
        shape like this:

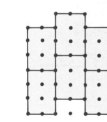

   (c) Do the same for all the other squares
        to produce a tessellation of cats.

2

   (a) Draw about 12 congruent
        rectangles like these.

   (b) Choose one rectangle and change
        its shape like this:

   (c) Do the same for all the other rectangles to produce a tessellation of dogs.

3 By altering each rectangle like this,
    convert a tessellation of rectangles
    to a tessellation of fish.

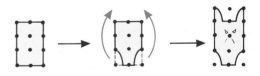

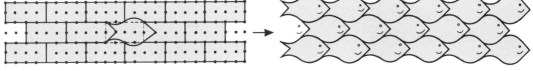

**1 You need a card rectangle 4 cm by 3 cm,
scissors and sticky tape.**

(a) Cut a piece out of one side.

(b) Stick it to the opposite side.

(c) Use your card shape as a template. Draw round it to
make a tessellation of about 12 faces.

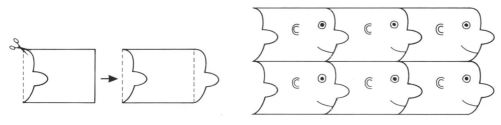

2 Take another card rectangle 4 cm by 3 cm. Make a template
like this:

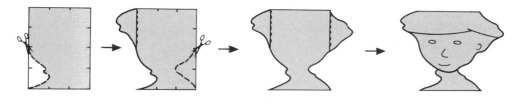

Draw round your template to make a tessellation like this:

3 Cut a triangle or a rectangle or a regular hexagon out of card.
Design a picture: cut off 2 or 3 pieces and stick them on again
to make a template. Use the template to draw a tessellation.

Challenge

4 Use an equilateral triangle. Make a template like this one.
Try to draw a tessellation like the one at the top of **Textbook page 21**.

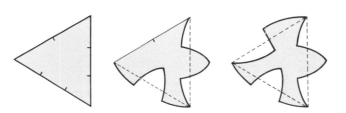

Ask your teacher what to do next.

1 Do Workbook pages 6 and 7.

Grady's Garden Centre sells shelves and plant pots. Each shelf holds 6 plant pots.

Number of shelves	1	2	3	4	5
Number of plant pots	6	12	18	24	30

The increase in the number of plant pots each time is **6**.

Formula:
The number of plant pots is **6** times the number of shelves.

The increase is the same number each time.

2 The garden centre grows plants under polythene supported by a metal frame. The frames are made from metal rods and plastic joints.
Here are frame sizes 1, 2 and 3.

Frame

Size 1   Size 2   Size 3

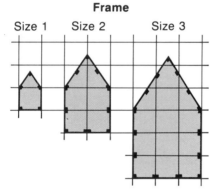

(a) Draw frame sizes 4 and 5.
(b) Copy and complete:

Frame size	1	2	3	4	5
Number of rods	5				

(c) What is the increase in the number of rods each time?
(d) Copy and complete this formula:
The number of rods is . . .

3 Grady's sells L-shaped goldfish ponds in a range of sizes.

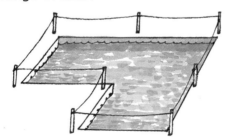

Here are the plans of the first two sizes.
The dots show where the fence posts go.

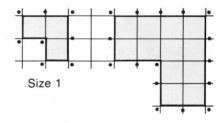

Size 1

Size 2

(a) Draw pond size 3 and mark the position of each post.
(b) Copy and complete:

Pond size	1	2	3	4
Number of posts				

(c) Write the formula for the number of posts.

1 Do Workbook page 8.

2 Grady's sells slabs which measure 1 m by 1 m.
Bert orders and lays slabs. Help him find a
formula to calculate how many slabs he
needs to surround **square** beds.

  (a) Draw diagrams to show paths
     around beds of side
     1 m, 2 m, 3 m and 4 m.

  (b) Copy and complete:

Breadth of bed in m	1	2	3	4
Number of slabs	8	12		

  (c) What is the increase in the number
     of slabs each time?

  (d) Copy and complete the formula:
     The number of slabs is . . .

  (e) Use the formula to find the number of slabs Bert
     needs for a square bed of side 7 m.
     Continue your table to check your answer.

3 Help Bert find a formula for **rectangular** beds when
the **length is 1 m more than the breadth**.

  (a) Draw diagrams to show paths
     around beds
     • 1 m broad by 2 m long
     • 2 m broad by 3 m long
     • 3 m broad by 4 m long
     • 4 m broad by 5 m long.

  (b) Copy and complete:

Breadth of bed in m	1	2	3	4
Number of slabs				

  (c) What is the increase in the number of slabs each time?

  (d) Write down the formula for the number of slabs.

  (e) Use the formula to find the number of slabs Bert
     needs for a bed of breadth 15 m.

4 (a) Find Bert's formula for rectangular beds when the **length
     is 2 m more than the breadth**.

Breadth of bed in m			
Number of slabs			

  (b) Use the formula to find the number of slabs Bert needs for a bed of breadth 22 m.

5 What size of **square** bed requires
  (a) 44 slabs **(b)** 100 slabs?

6 Investigate the dimensions of all square and rectangular beds which require 20 slabs.

Challenge

Investigation

At Raji's Tandoori Restaurant, there are groups of small tables along one wall like this:

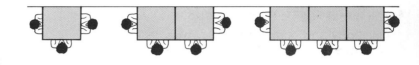

1 How many people can sit at a group of **(a)** 4 tables **(b)** 5 tables?

2 Copy and complete:

Number of tables	1	2	3		
Number of seats					

3 What is the increase in the number of seats each time?

Formula: The number of seats is **1** times the number of tables then **add 2**.
 or   The number of seats is the number of tables then add 2.

4 How many people can sit at a group of
(a) 9 tables **(b)** 11 tables?

Raji has put groups of larger tables along another wall.

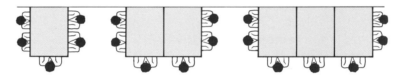

5 How many people can sit at a group of **(a)** 4 tables **(b)** 5 tables?

6 Copy and complete:

Number of tables	1	2	3		
Number of seats					

7 (a) What is the increase in the number of seats each time?
 (b) Write the formula for the number of seats.

8 How many people can sit at a group of **(a)** 8 tables **(b)** 10 tables?

Other tables are arranged like this:

9 How many people can sit at a group of **(a)** 4 tables **(b)** 5 tables?

10 Copy and complete:

Number of tables	1	2	3		
Number of seats					

11 (a) What is the increase in the number of seats each time?
 (b) Write the formula for the number of seats.

12 How many people can sit at a group of **(a)** 10 tables **(b)** 12 tables?

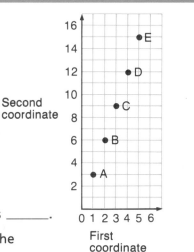

1 A is the point (1, 3). B is the point (2, 6).

(a) Copy and complete this **coordinate table**
for points A to E.

	A	B	C	D	E
First coordinate	1	2			
Second coordinate	3	6			

Second
coordinate

First
coordinate

(b) Copy and complete:

The increase in the second coordinate each time is _____.

Formula: The second coordinate is _____ times the
first coordinate.

2 For each of these sets of points • draw a coordinate table • write a formula.

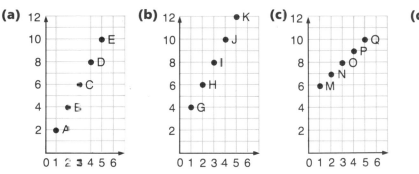

**3 Work with a partner. You need a grid like this
and two differently coloured dice, say one red
and one blue.**

The red die gives the first coordinate and the blue die
gives the second coordinate.

One player marks points with a cross —✳— and the
other with a circle —⊕—. Take turns to throw the two
dice and mark the points on the grid.

The winner is the first to mark any four points which
are the corners of a square.

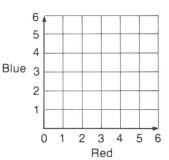

Blue

Red

4 You can draw the square in the
diagram by joining points like this:

(a) Draw four different squares, each
on a separate coordinate grid.

(b) List the coordinates of
the corners of each square like this:

(c) List the coordinates of another
square without drawing it.

(d) Copy and complete these lists of coordinates for squares:

(2,5) ← (5,5)
↓   ↑
(2,2) → (5,2)

(,) ← (,)
↓   ↑
(,) → (,)

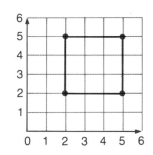

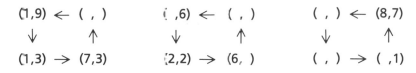

(1,9) ← (,)
↓   ↑
(1,3) → (7,3)

(,6) ← (,)
↓   ↑
(2,2) → (6,)

(,) ← (8,7)
↓   ↑
(,) → (,1)

You can use coordinates to design repeating patterns for wallpaper or fabric.

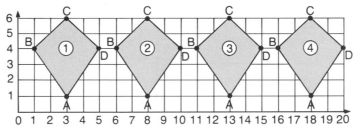

1 (a) Copy and complete this table which shows the coordinates of the corners of each kite.

(b) Extend your table for a fifth kite. Explain how to find the coordinates for the fifth kite without drawing it.

	Corner			
Kite	A	B	C	D
①	(3, 1)	(1, 4)	(3, 6)	(5, 4)
②				
③				
④				

2 (a) Copy this table. Put in the coordinates of the corners of arrow shape 1.

	Corner						
Arrow	A	B	C	D	E	F	G
①	(3,1)						
②	(3,7)						
③							
④							

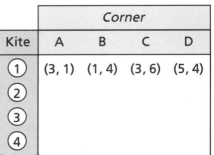

(b) To make a new arrow increase all the **second coordinates** by 6. Complete your table for three new arrows.

(c) Show all four arrows on a coordinate diagram.

3 (a) Draw each shape in the table on the same coordinate diagram by joining the points in this order:

Shape	Corner				
①	(2, 1) →	(2, 4) →	(1, 4) →	(1, 3) →	(4, 3)
②	(4, 3) →	(4, 6) →	(3, 6) →	(3, 5) →	(6, 5)
③	(6, 5) →	(6, 8) →	(5, 8) →	(5, 7) →	(8, 7)
④	(8, 7) →	(8, 10) →	(7, 10) →	(7, 9) →	(10, 9)

(b) For each shape describe how the **first coordinate** changes.

(c) Repeat **(b)** for the second coordinates.

(d) Without drawing it, list the coordinates for each corner of the fifth shape.

Ask your teacher what to do next.

This computer graphics image based on an equilateral triangle is made by plotting lots of coordinates on a screen.

Lifescapes Exhibition Centre

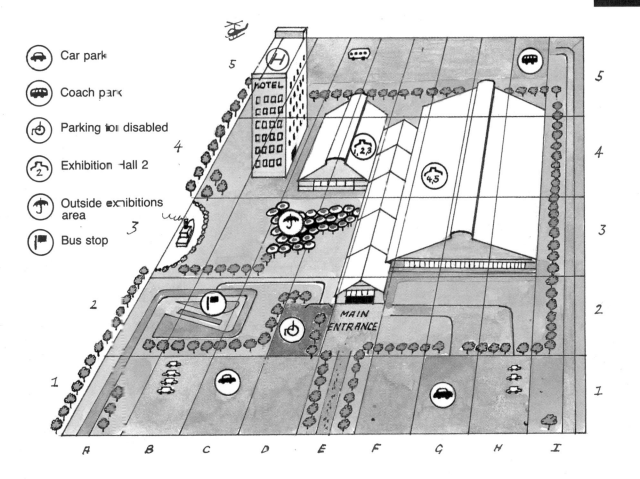

- 🚗 Car park
- 🚌 Coach park
- ♿ Parking for disabled
- Exhibition Hall 2
- Outside exhibitions area
- Bus stop

This is a plan of the new Lifescapes Exhibition Centre.

1 🚗 shows the position of a car park on the plan.
There is a car park at **G1**. What is shown by the symbol at
(a) H5 **(b)** D4 **(c)** B2 **(d)** C1 **(e)** C3?

2 What is the position of
  (a) the main entrance
  (b) the car park for disabled people
  (c) the hotel door
  (d) the boat
  (e) the symbol for Halls 4 and 5?

3 Do you think the car park for the disabled is
in a good position? Explain your answer.

4 The total floor area of Exhibition Halls 4 and 5
is about 15 000 m². By looking at the plan,
estimate the total floor area of Halls 1, 2 and 3.

5 (a) What is the area of your classroom floor in m²?
  (b) About how many times does this area fit into
    the total floor area of Halls 4 and 5?

The Halls at Lifescapes

1 Lifescapes Exhibition Centre has five halls. Read about them in this extract from the brochure.

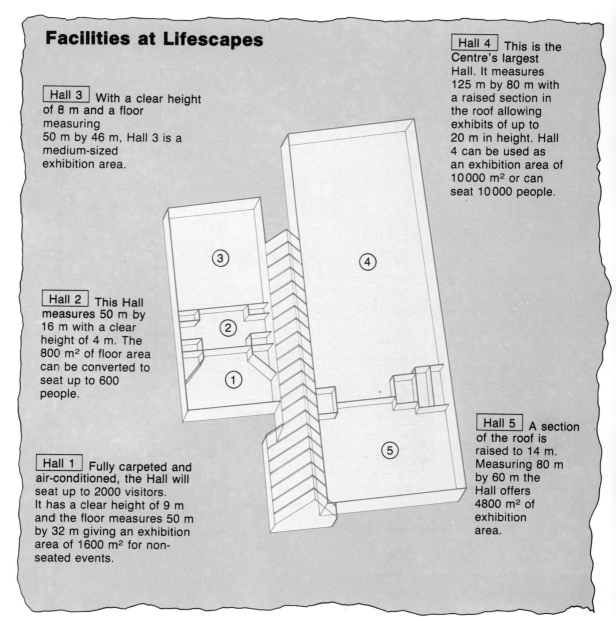

Facilities at Lifescapes

Hall 3 With a clear height of 8 m and a floor measuring 50 m by 46 m, Hall 3 is a medium-sized exhibition area.

Hall 2 This Hall measures 50 m by 16 m with a clear height of 4 m. The 800 m² of floor area can be converted to seat up to 600 people.

Hall 1 Fully carpeted and air-conditioned, the Hall will seat up to 2000 visitors. It has a clear height of 9 m and the floor measures 50 m by 32 m giving an exhibition area of 1600 m² for non-seated events.

Hall 4 This is the Centre's largest Hall. It measures 125 m by 80 m with a raised section in the roof allowing exhibits of up to 20 m in height. Hall 4 can be used as an exhibition area of 10 000 m² or can seat 10 000 people.

Hall 5 A section of the roof is raised to 14 m. Measuring 80 m by 60 m the Hall offers 4800 m² of exhibition area.

2 Megan works in the Information Centre at Lifescapes. She needs to find information about the halls quickly. Copy and complete this table for her.

	Height	Length	Breadth	Area	Seating capacity
Hall 1	9 m	50	32	1600 m²	2000
Hall 2	4	50	16	800 m²	600
Hall 3	8	50	46	2309	
Hall 4	20	120	80	10000 m²	10 000
Hall 5	14	80	60	4800	

Forthcoming attractions

Four events are to be held at Lifescapes on 2nd December.
They each need a different hall.

Ice hockey
The rink measures 22 m by 66 m.

Circus
The trapeze needs to be 17 m from the ground.

Fabric and fashion
This exhibition will be held in a hall which has a floor area of at least 2000 m².

Ballet
A ballet company has booked a hall which can seat 1000 people.

Megan has to program the events board so people can see which hall to go to.

1 (a) Decide which event should go in each hall. Copy and complete the board.

(b) Write the reasons for your decisions.

(c) Which hall is not booked?

```
WELCOME TO LIFESCAPES EXHIBITION CENTRE

HALL 1    _____
HALL 2    _____
HALL 3    _____
HALL 4    _____
HALL 5    _____
```

2 All four events will be at Lifescapes on 2nd December, but they start and finish on different dates. Copy and complete the table for Megan's records.

Event	Hall number	Starting date	Number of days	Finishing date
Ice hockey		28 Nov	6	
Fabric and fashion		1 Dec	4	
Ballet			3	2 Dec
Circus		18 Nov		5 Dec

At the moment, only these four events are booked in at Lifescapes during December.

3 (a) Read this letter from the secretary of White Peaks Ski Club.

(b) Write a reply from the manager to Mrs White. In your letter:
- explain why the Ski Show cannot start on 1st December
- list the suitable halls with the date that each becomes available
- name the hall and date you think she should choose. Give her a reason for your decision.

4 Mrs White agrees with your choice. Design and colour a poster advertising the Ski Show.

WHITE PEAKS SKI CLUB
21 HILLVIEW, AVIEMORE

The Manager
Lifescapes Exhibition Centre

Dear Sir or Madam

It is White Peaks Ski Club's tenth anniversary on 1st December. To celebrate, we would like to hold a three-day Ski Show at the Lifescapes Centre, starting on this date.

We want to give visitors to our show a chance to try skiing on a dry ski-slope. We need a hall which has a length of at least 20 m and a minimum clear height of 12 m.

Yours faithfully

R White

MRS R WHITE
SECRETARY

Diary of events

Lifescapes Centre is busy during the month of January. Megan has a wallchart to keep track of events.

> The Antiques Roadshow will be held in Hall 3 from 15th to 18th January.

JAN	1	2	3	4	5	6	7	8	9	10	11	12	13	14	15	16	17	18	19	20	21	22	23	24	25	26	27	28	29	30	31
HALL 1					YOUTH THEATRE					CARTOON FESTIVAL									WORLD AID					JUDO COMPETITION							
HALL 2		RADIO ROADSHOW							FLOWER SHOW				RSPCA			CHRISTIAN EXHIBITION				HEALTHY LIVING								BOOK CLUB			
HALL 3			CAT SHOW						HOLIDAY EXHIBITION				WINE FESTIVAL			ANTIQUES ROADSHOW					FABRIC + FASHION				CAREERS CONVENTION						
HALL 4		RNLI		PRINTING SHOW		SIX-A-SIDE FOOTBALL				TECHNOLOGY WEEK						CAMPING + CARAVANNING					MICRO-COMPUTERS				CAREERS CONVENTION						
HALL 5		ENERGY SHOW		WINDSURFING EXHIBITION			KIDS ONLY								CARNIVAL												POP CONCERT				

1 Which event will be held in Hall 1 from 19th to 23rd January?

2 Write which halls and dates are booked for these events:
- **(a)** Cartoon Festival
- **(b)** Kids Only
- **(c)** Radio Roadshow
- **(d)** RSPCA
- **(e)** Youth Theatre
- **(f)** Careers Convention.

3 List the events, if any, which will be held in each hall on
- **(a)** 14th January
- **(b)** 21st January.

4 (a) For how many days in January is Hall 3 empty?
(b) On which day are all the halls empty? Why do you think this is?

5 The Carnival starts on a Friday. On which day of the week does
(a) the Carnival end **(b)** the Flower Show start?

6 The Reverend Brown wants to see both World Aid and the Christian Exhibition. On which dates could he go and see both?

7 Mrs Scott is going to the Holiday Exhibition. Her son David would like to see the Six-a-Side Football and her daughter Samantha wants to go to the Windsurfing Exhibition. When do you think the family should visit the Centre?

8 Alex, Duncan and Talat want to visit the Centre together but they cannot agree on a date.

Alex wants to see the Judo competition
Duncan is interested in the Book Club
Talat would like to find out about microcomputers.

The boys could visit the Centre on 24th or 25th January and disappoint Duncan.
- **(a)** Who would be disappointed if they visited the Centre on 29th or 30th January?
- **(b)** List the other dates which the boys might choose and say who would be disappointed.

 9 Do Workbook page 9.

What's on today

You need isometric paper.

1 Lifescapes held a competition
to design a badge for
the Exhibition Centre.

Here is one entry:

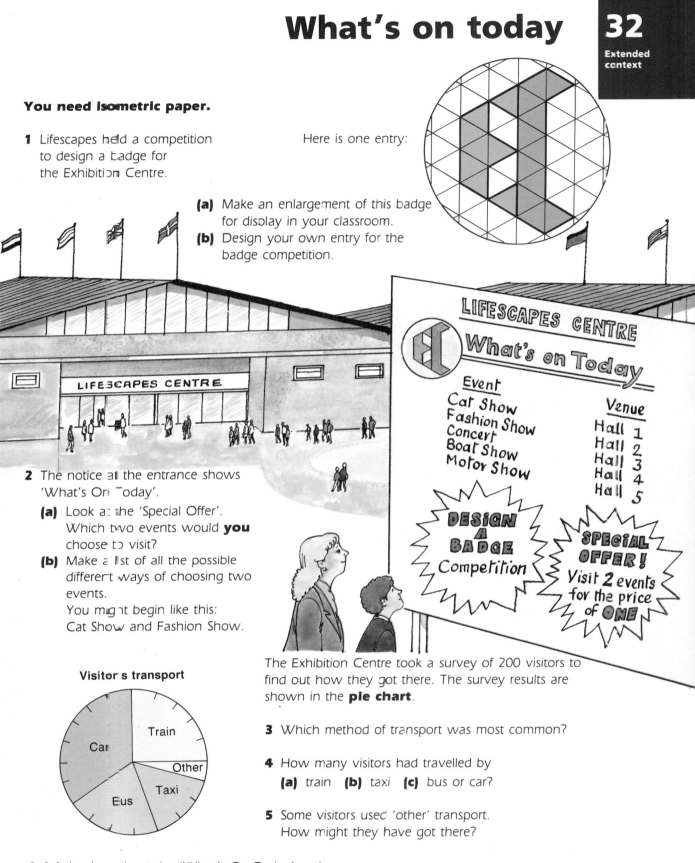

(a) Make an enlargement of this badge
for display in your classroom.

(b) Design your own entry for the
badge competition.

2 The notice at the entrance shows
'What's On Today'.

(a) Look at the 'Special Offer'.
Which two events would **you**
choose to visit?

(b) Make a list of all the possible
different ways of choosing two
events.
You might begin like this:
Cat Show and Fashion Show.

Visitor's transport

The Exhibition Centre took a survey of 200 visitors to
find out how they got there. The survey results are
shown in the **pie chart**.

3 Which method of transport was most common?

4 How many visitors had travelled by
(a) train **(b)** taxi **(c)** bus or car?

5 Some visitors used 'other' transport.
How might they have got there?

6 (a) Look again at the 'What's On Today' notice.
Which **one** of the events would you **most** like to visit?

(b) Carry out a survey of your own class.
Find out which **one** of the five events each pupil would
most like to visit.
Draw a **bar chart** to show your results.

Basketball competition

You are the captain of a basketball team which has entered a competition.
Your team has to play against five other teams in a local league.
The top team will go through to the finals at Lifescapes Exhibition Centre.

The local league

You need Workbook page 10.

1 (a) Choose a name for your team. Write the name of your team on the coloured rectangles in the list of results.

(b) Each team plays every other team **once** only. Complete the names of the teams missing from the Thursday and Friday games.

2 Each team gets 2 league points for a win and 0 points when they lose. Complete the table for the number of league points for each team.

3 When two teams have the same number of league points, the one with the greater **difference** between total score **for** and total score **against** is placed first. Complete the league table.

4 Which team

(a) qualified for the finals   **(b)** had the highest total score **for**?

5 Calculate the average score per game **for** each team.

6 (a) The Health Education Council sponsored this league.
The prize money in pounds was equal to the total score of all the matches. How much was this?

(b) The first three teams, in order, received $\frac{1}{2}$, $\frac{1}{4}$, $\frac{1}{5}$ of the prize money. Make a list of these teams and their prize money.

(c) The fourth team received the remaining prize money. How much was this?

The basketball finals

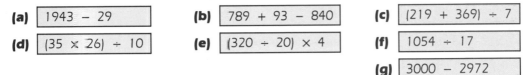

There are eight teams, including your own, in the basketball finals.
The finals are run as a knock-out competition.

You need Workbook page 11.

1 (a) Ask pupils in your class for the names of seven other qualifying teams. Write the names on slips of paper.

(b) Make a draw for the quarter-finals and write the names of the teams in the boxes.

Quarter-finals

2 (a) Use a calculator to find $\boxed{1288 \div 14}$

(b) Enter the answer as your team's score in the quarter-finals.

3 The answers to these calculations are the scores for the other seven teams. Enter them in order on the results sheet.

(a) $\boxed{1943 - 29}$ **(b)** $\boxed{789 + 93 - 840}$ **(c)** $\boxed{(219 + 369) \div 7}$

(d) $\boxed{(35 \times 26) \div 10}$ **(e)** $\boxed{(320 \div 20) \times 4}$ **(f)** $\boxed{1054 \div 17}$

(g) $\boxed{3000 - 2972}$

4 Put the names of the winning teams into the semi-finals.

Semi-finals

In basketball, a goal scores 2 and a free throw scores 1.

5 (a) Your team scores $\boxed{37 \text{ goals and } 11 \text{ free throws}}$ in the semi-final.
Enter your team's score.

(b) There is only one point between your team and your opponents in the semi-final. Their score is made up of an equal number of goals and free throws.
How many goals do they score? Enter their total score.

(c) Give the remaining two teams these scores:
$\boxed{19 \text{ goals and } 9 \text{ free throws}}$ $\boxed{27 \text{ goals and } 6 \text{ free throws}}$

6 Enter the names of the finalists.

The final

7 Fill in the report of the final for the *Daily News*.

8 There are two minutes to go in the final. The score is 64–64. Toss a coin to decide which team scores the last 2 points. Complete the report of the final.

Fabric and Fashion Exhibition

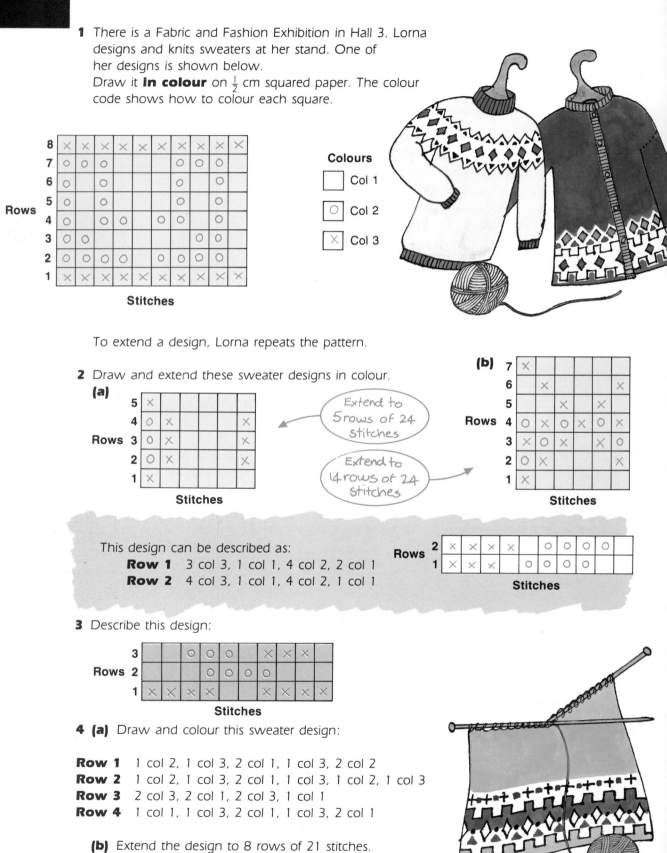

1 There is a Fabric and Fashion Exhibition in Hall 3. Lorna designs and knits sweaters at her stand. One of her designs is shown below.
Draw it **in colour** on $\frac{1}{2}$ cm squared paper. The colour code shows how to colour each square.

Colours

- ☐ Col 1
- ⊙ Col 2
- ☒ Col 3

Rows / Stitches

To extend a design, Lorna repeats the pattern.

2 Draw and extend these sweater designs in colour.

(a) Rows / Stitches

Extend to 5 rows of 24 stitches

Extend to 14 rows of 24 stitches

(b) Rows / Stitches

This design can be described as:
Row 1 3 col 3, 1 col 1, 4 col 2, 2 col 1
Row 2 4 col 3, 1 col 1, 4 col 2, 1 col 1

Rows / Stitches

3 Describe this design:

Rows / Stitches

4 **(a)** Draw and colour this sweater design:

Row 1 1 col 2, 1 col 3, 2 col 1, 1 col 3, 2 col 2
Row 2 1 col 2, 1 col 3, 2 col 1, 1 col 3, 1 col 2, 1 col 3
Row 3 2 col 3, 2 col 1, 2 col 3, 1 col 1
Row 4 1 col 1, 1 col 3, 2 col 1, 1 col 3, 2 col 1

(b) Extend the design to 8 rows of 21 stitches.

5 Draw and describe a design of your own.

Rajesh has a stand at the Fabric and Fashion Exhibition.
He prints T-shirts for customers with their own designs.

You need Workbook page 22. Make these T-shirt designs.

6 (a) Cut out the triangle.

(b) Cut along the dotted lines and **slide** each shape.

(c) Draw, cut out and slide more shapes. Glue them on coloured paper.

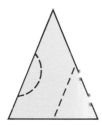
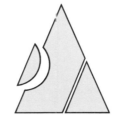

7 (a) Cut out the circle.

(b) Cut along the dotted lines and **flip** each shape over.

(c) Draw, cut out and flip more shapes. Glue them on coloured paper.

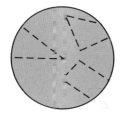
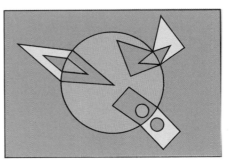

8 You can combine sliding and flipping to make designs like the ones below.

(a) Cut out the rectangle and square.

(b) Make your own T-shirt designs by sliding and flipping shapes.

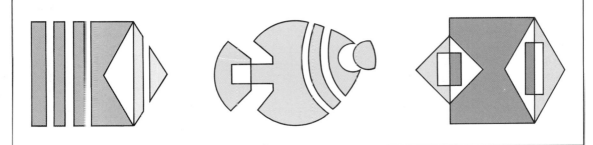

Judo

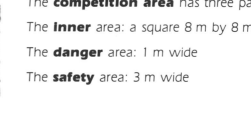

There is a Judo Competition at Lifescapes.
The **competition area** has three parts.

The **inner** area: a square 8 m by 8 m

The **danger** area: 1 m wide

The **safety** area: 3 m wide

You need Workbook page 12.

1 (a) The plan in the workbook shows Hall 1. Use the scale given and draw a complete competition area with the **X** as its centre.

(b) Colour the competition area as shown. ———————►

2 The Centre uses mats measuring 2 m by 1 m for the competition area. Use your plan to find the number of
(a) green mats   **(b)** red mats   **(c)** blue mats.

3 The red and green parts together form the **contest area**. What is its true length and breadth?

4 Draw as many contest areas as you can on your plan.
- Each contest area must have a blue 3 m safety area around it.
- Safety areas may be shared.

5 The positions of some seats are marked on your plan. Which doors are nearest to the following seats?
(a) Z1   **(b)** A7   **(c)** E33
(d) W12   **(e)** C43   **(f)** W39

6 George's seat is G3. It is marked on your plan like this: [G] .
In the same way mark seats for
(a) Dorothy, D22   **(b)** Marion, M5
(c) Tom, T4.

7 The attendant told Tom the best way to find his seat.

Copy and complete the instructions for Tom.

'Go in through door 3. Turn _____. Go to the end of the hall and turn _____. Take the first passageway on your _____. Your seat is the _____ one along in the _____ row on your _____.'

8 Use the scale given and a ruler. Find in metres the shortest distance from:

(a) Dorothy to the centre **X**

(b) Marion to the centre **X**

(c) Dorothy to Marion.

9 Seats for the Judo Competition cost £7 and £10. The £10 seats are seats 13 to 36 in rows A to E and V to Z

(a) Colour these seats on your plan.

(b) Why do you think these seats cost more than the others?

10 Megan kept a record of seat bookings for the Judo Competition. 'Claws' escaped from the Cat Show and ate part of the record.

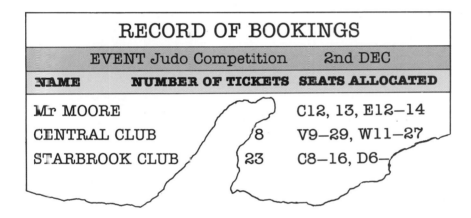

RECORD OF BOOKINGS		
EVENT Judo Competition		2nd DEC
NAME	NUMBER OF TICKETS	SEATS ALLOCATED
Mr MOORE		C12, 13, E12–14
CENTRAL CLUB	8	V9–29, W11–27
STARBROOK CLUB	23	C8–16, D6–

(a) How many seats did Mr Moore book? How much did he pay?

(b) How many seats did the Central Club book?

(c) The Starbrook Club booked seats in rows C and D. Which seats did they book in row D?

11 Joyce Chung paid £65 for 8 seats. How many £10 seats and £7 seats did she book?

12 (a) How many seats are in the hall?

(b) How many of these seats are £10 seats?

(c) How much was collected from ticket sales for the finals?

JUDO COMPETITION FINALS — SOLD OUT

13 The cleaner found an umbrella under seat W22. How could the Lost Property Office find who owns it?

14 The cleaners have handed in all the keys. Which keys have been hung in the wrong place?

Lifescapes car parks

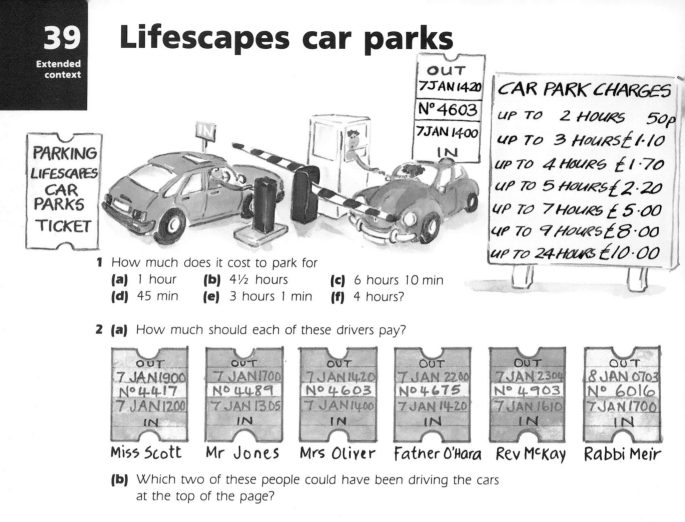

CAR PARK CHARGES

UP TO	2 HOURS	50p
UP TO	3 HOURS	£1·10
UP TO	4 HOURS	£1·70
UP TO	5 HOURS	£2·20
UP TO	7 HOURS	£5·00
UP TO	9 HOURS	£8·00
UP TO	24 HOURS	£10·00

1 How much does it cost to park for
   (a) 1 hour   (b) 4½ hours   (c) 6 hours 10 min
   (d) 45 min   (e) 3 hours 1 min   (f) 4 hours?

2 (a) How much should each of these drivers pay?

Miss Scott — OUT 7 JAN 1900 N° 4417 7 JAN 1200 IN
Mr Jones — OUT 7 JAN 1700 N° 4489 7 JAN 1305 IN
Mrs Oliver — OUT 7 JAN 1420 N° 4603 7 JAN 1400 IN
Father O'Hara — OUT 7 JAN 2200 N° 4675 7 JAN 1420 IN
Rev McKay — OUT 7 JAN 2304 N° 4903 7 JAN 1610 IN
Rabbi Meir — OUT 8 JAN 0703 N° 6016 7 JAN 1700 IN

   (b) Which two of these people could have been driving the cars
       at the top of the page?

3 Look at the ticket numbers. How many cars went into the car park
   from 2 pm to 5 pm?

4 Mr Martin came to see the Windsurfing Exhibition. He drove into
   the car park at 9 am. He drove out at 1.25 pm. How much should
   he pay for parking?

5 Mr Singh drove into the car park at half-past three. When he
   drove out he was charged £1·70.
   Write   (a) the latest   (b) the earliest time he could have driven
   out of the car park.

6 Copy and complete this table:

Name	Time in	Parking charge	Time out Latest	Time out Earliest
Mrs Thomas	1250	£2·20	1750	1651
Mr Coburg	1433	£1·70		
Miss Wong		£5	1944	

7 The car park attendant puts used
   tickets in a box. Use a calculator to
   find the total takings for the day.

210   75   52   1
140   112   44

| 50p | £1·10 | £1·70 | £2·20 | £5 | £8 | £10 |

Ask your teacher what to do next.

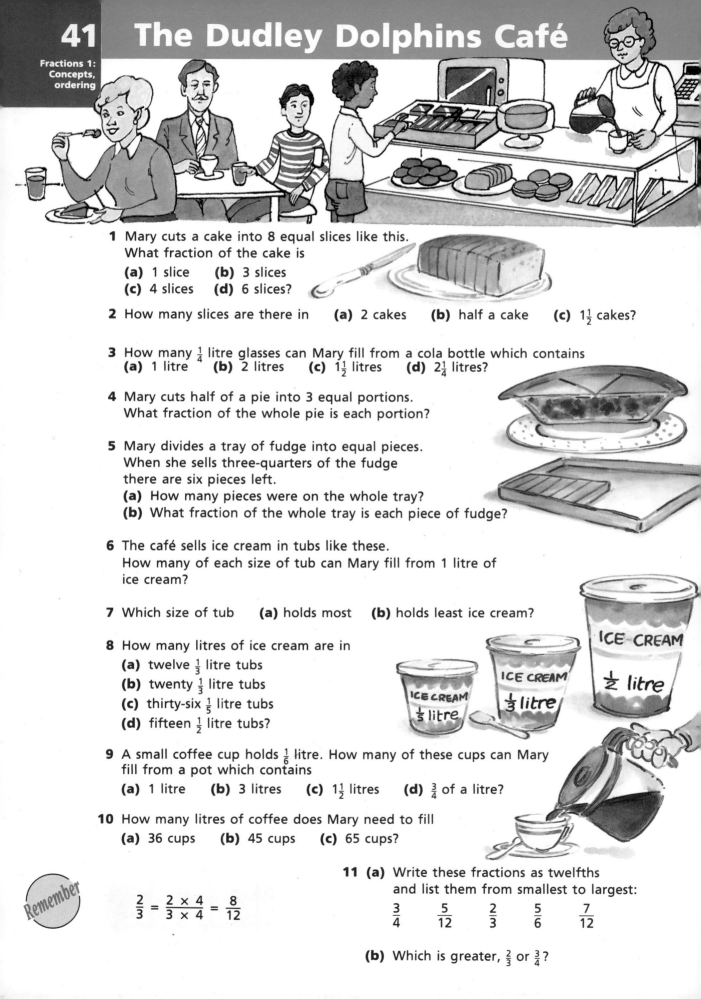

1 Mary cuts a cake into 8 equal slices like this.
What fraction of the cake is
   (a) 1 slice   **(b)** 3 slices
   (c) 4 slices   **(d)** 6 slices?

2 How many slices are there in   **(a)** 2 cakes   **(b)** half a cake   **(c)** $1\frac{1}{2}$ cakes?

3 How many $\frac{1}{4}$ litre glasses can Mary fill from a cola bottle which contains
   (a) 1 litre   **(b)** 2 litres   **(c)** $1\frac{1}{2}$ litres   **(d)** $2\frac{1}{4}$ litres?

4 Mary cuts half of a pie into 3 equal portions.
What fraction of the whole pie is each portion?

5 Mary divides a tray of fudge into equal pieces.
When she sells three-quarters of the fudge
there are six pieces left.
   (a) How many pieces were on the whole tray?
   (b) What fraction of the whole tray is each piece of fudge?

6 The café sells ice cream in tubs like these.
How many of each size of tub can Mary fill from 1 litre of
ice cream?

7 Which size of tub   **(a)** holds most   **(b)** holds least ice cream?

8 How many litres of ice cream are in
   (a) twelve $\frac{1}{3}$ litre tubs
   (b) twenty $\frac{1}{3}$ litre tubs
   (c) thirty-six $\frac{1}{5}$ litre tubs
   (d) fifteen $\frac{1}{2}$ litre tubs?

9 A small coffee cup holds $\frac{1}{6}$ litre. How many of these cups can Mary
fill from a pot which contains
   (a) 1 litre   **(b)** 3 litres   **(c)** $1\frac{1}{2}$ litres   **(d)** $\frac{3}{4}$ of a litre?

10 How many litres of coffee does Mary need to fill
   (a) 36 cups   **(b)** 45 cups   **(c)** 65 cups?

Remember

$$\frac{2}{3} = \frac{2 \times 4}{3 \times 4} = \frac{8}{12}$$

11 (a) Write these fractions as twelfths
and list them from smallest to largest:

   $\frac{3}{4}$ $\frac{5}{12}$ $\frac{2}{3}$ $\frac{5}{6}$ $\frac{7}{12}$

(b) Which is greater, $\frac{2}{3}$ or $\frac{3}{4}$?

The Dudley Dolphins Swimming Club has 60 members.
15 out of the 60 members are juniors.

The fraction of the members who are juniors is

$$\frac{15}{60} = \frac{3}{12} = \frac{1}{4}$$

with $\div 5$ and $\div 3$ applied to numerator and denominator.

To simplify a fraction divide both numerator and denominator by the same number.

$\frac{1}{4}$ of the members are juniors.

$\frac{3}{4}$ of the members are **not** juniors.

1 The Club has 20 male members. Find in simplest form the fraction of the members who are
   (a) males   **(b)** females.

2 The Club has 24 sprint swimmers. Find in simplest form the fraction of the members who are
   (a) sprint swimmers   **(b)** not sprint swimmers.

3 In the Club's first five years, the fractions of the members who were male were

year 1 $\frac{30}{50}$ year 2 $\frac{20}{48}$ year 3 $\frac{27}{54}$ year 4 $\frac{21}{56}$ year 5 $\frac{42}{60}$

For each year
   (a) simplify the fraction who were male
   (b) give the fraction who were female.

4 In which of these years was the **fraction** who were male
   (a) less than $\frac{1}{2}$ **(b)** greatest?

CLUB ROOM SNACKS

Table 1

drinks	25p
biscuits	15p
crisps	20p
TOTAL	**60p**

At Table 1, 25p out of 60p was spent on drinks.
The **fraction** of the total spent on drinks was

$$\frac{25p}{60p} = \frac{25}{60} = \frac{5}{12}$$

5 Find in simplest form the fraction spent on
   (a) biscuits   **(b)** crisps.

6 For each of these bills find the fraction of the total spent on
   (a) drinks
   (b) biscuits
   (c) crisps.

CLUB ROOM SNACKS

Table 2

drinks	36p
biscuits	30p
crisps	24p
TOTAL	90p

CLUB ROOM SNACKS

Table 3

drinks	30p
biscuits	24p
crisps	26p
TOTAL	80p

CLUB ROOM SNACKS

Table 4

drinks	40p
biscuits	48p
crisps	32p
TOTAL	£1.20

1 Pupils from five local primary schools go on to Strangehill Secondary. Mrs Wong, the headteacher at Strangehill, wants information about **next** year's intake of pupils. She sends a questionnaire to each local school. Discuss with your group which questions she might ask.

Mrs Wong wants to display some of her questionnaire results as bar graphs (bar charts).

How many pupils are coming to Strangehill?		
School	Boys	Girls
Croftbank (C)	20	23
Gladeside (G)	14	16
Learnwell (L)	31	21
Parkland (P)	8	15
Roseside (R)	10	7

Here is part of the bar graph.

The bar graph has a title.

Each axis is labelled.

You need Workbook page 13.

2 Complete **Graph 1**.

3 The total number of pupils from Croftbank is 43.
 (a) Calculate the total number of pupils coming from each school.
 (b) Show this information on **Graph 2**.

What will these pupils do for lunch?				
School	School lunch (L)	Packed lunch (P)	Home (H)	Cafe (c)
Croftbank	14	12	4	13
Gladeside	8	9	5	8
Learnwell	19	16	10	7
Parkland	6	9	3	5
Roseside	5	4	5	3

 (a) Show the information for Croftbank and Parkland on **Graphs 3 and 4**.
 (b) Fifty-two pupils have chosen to take school lunches.
  Show the total for each choice on **Graph 5**.

5

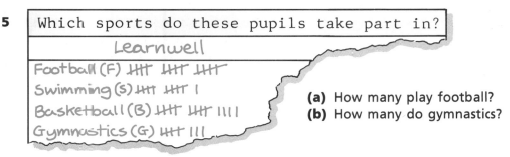

Which sports do these pupils take part in?

Learnwell

Football (F) ⅢⅢ ⅢⅢ ⅢⅢ
Swimming (S) ⅢⅢ ⅢⅢ I
Basketball (B) ⅢⅢ ⅢⅢ IIII
Gymnastics (G) ⅢⅢ III

(a) How many play football?

(b) How many do gymnastics?

(c) **Go to Workbook page 14** and show this information on **Graph 6**.

6 Collect information about your classmates' favourite sports.
Use the information to draw a bar graph like **Graph 6**.

Mrs Wong asked each school about
pupil absence in the summer term.
The table shows the number of
pupils absent each day.

Pupil absence					
Summer term	M	Tu	W	Th	F
Week 1	✕	✕	12	9	9
Week 2	5	6	8	6	5
Week 3	7	9	7	7	10
Week 4	10	12	16	17	16
Week 5	✕	17	16	15	15
Week 6	15	12	10	8	9
Week 7	9	7	8	7	10
Week 8	8	10	✕	✕	✕

✕ School holiday

During week 4
• the highest number of absences = 17
• the lowest number of absences = 10
• the **range** of absences = 17 − 10 = **7**

The **range** is the
difference between
the highest and lowest values.

7 Find the range of absences for

(a) each of the other weeks **(b)** the whole summer term.

To find the **mean** or **average** daily absence in **week 4**,
add up the **5** numbers then divide by **5**.

Enter `10` Press `+` `1` `2` `+` `1` `6` `+` `1` `7` `+` `1` `6` `=`

to give `71` Press `÷` `5` `=` to give `14.2`

The **mean** daily absence in week 4 is 14 **to the nearest whole number**.

8 (a) Calculate the **mean** daily absence for each of the other
weeks. Round each answer to the nearest whole number.

(b) **Go to Workbook page 14** and complete **Graph 7**.

(c) During the term there was a flu epidemic. In which week
was it worst?

1 These are the weights to the nearest kilogram of the pupils in class 2:

```
37  41  28  42  33  38  34  29  39  54
51  38  39  35  42  35  37  43  24  47
41  30  50  40  36  33  46  42  38  45
```

(a) Find the range of weights.
(b) Copy and complete this **frequency table**.
(c) **Go to Workbook page 14** and show this information on **Graph 8**.
(d) How many pupils were weighed?
(e) Which **weight interval** contains most pupils?
(f) How many pupils weigh 40 kg or more?

Weight interval in kg	Tally marks	Frequency
20–24		
25–29		
30–34		
35–39		
40–44		
45–49		
50–54		

2 These are the heights to the nearest centimetre of the pupils in class 2:

```
138  140  155  144  152  148  142  136  153  160
154  137  139  146  162  165  154  132  153  157
159  172  143  129  146  168  149  135  147  144
```

(a) Find the range of heights.
(b) Copy and complete this **frequency table**.
(c) **Go to Workbook page 14** and show this information on **Graph 9**.
(d) Which **height interval** contains fewest pupils?
(e) How many pupils are shorter than 150 cm?

Height interval in cm	Tally marks	Frequency
120–129		
130–139		
140–149		
150–159		
160–169		
170–179		

3 Steven Ashley joins class 2. He weighs 52 kg and is 181 cm tall.
Write **(a)** his weight interval **(b)** his height interval.

4 (a) Find to the nearest kilogram the weights of pupils in your class.
   • Make a frequency table.
   • Show this information on a bar graph.
   Remember to number and label each axis and to give the graph a title.
(b) Find to the nearest centimetre the heights of pupils in your class. Make a frequency table and show this information on a graph.

1 Each bar graph shows the **same** results from the September test.

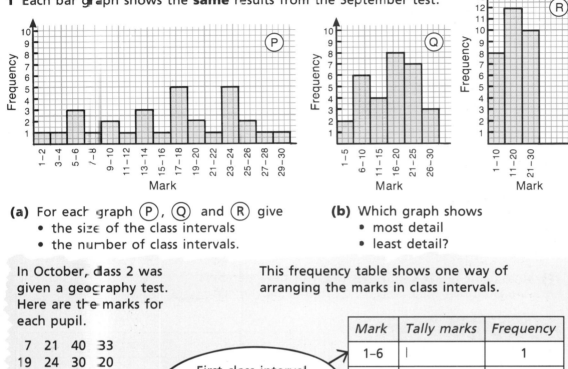

(a) For each graph (P), (Q) and (R) give
- the size of the class intervals
- the number of class intervals.

(b) Which graph shows
- most detail
- least detail?

In October, class 2 was given a geography test. Here are the marks for each pupil.

7	21	40	33
19	24	30	20
13	39	12	25
38	27	15	4
28	25	19	31
27	17	24	25

This frequency table shows one way of arranging the marks in class intervals.

First class interval contains lowest mark

Last class interval contains highest mark

Mark	Tally marks	Frequency
1–6	I	1
7–12	II	2
13–18	IIII	4
19–24	卌	5
25–30	卌 II	7
31–36	II	2
37–42	III	3

2 Make a frequency table which shows another way of arranging the October test marks.

3 For each test in this table
  (a) find the **range**
  (b) list suitable class intervals. Try to have from 5 to 12 class intervals.

	Class 2 tests		
	French	Maths	Science
Lowest mark	3	21	43
Highest mark	32	94	185

4 For each set of marks make a frequency table with class intervals and draw a bar graph.

Class 2 November test

12	14	11	7	10	4
8	13	10	11	6	11
16	14	5	16	15	12
11	13	10	9	11	18
9	10	14	6	13	19

Class 2 End-of-term test

31	17	42	28	35
18	24	39	13	41
41	21	31	43	32
40	19	22	35	39
27	44	17	19	26
16	38	32	47	21

Strangehill Secondary School Class 2 Final Exam Results

74	88	114	91	37	148
56	128	134	100	125	96
69	105	139	56	77	118
117	61	48	116	135	20
41	127	105	31	89	86

You can **count** or **measure** statistical data. You can count the number of **people** in the Strangehill Sports Club. You can measure the **distance** Jo throws the discus.

1 Which of the following can you
  • count   • measure?
  (a) the **time** taken to swim 50 metres
  (b) the **number of runners** in a race
  (c) the **spectators** in a stadium
  (d) the **depth** of a swimming pool
  (e) the **weight** of a barbell
  (f) the **money** taken at the gates.

The Strangehill Sports Club holds trials for new members.
Here are the times measured for 25 runners in the 100-metres sprint.

Time in seconds

12·4	13·2	12·6	13·1	11·8
11·5	12·4	13·2	12·0	12·3
12·4	13·0	12·2	11·0	11·9
10·9	11·1	12·5	11·0	13·0
13·1	12·8	11·0	12·5	11·4

You can use a frequency table like this when data is measured. The class interval **10·5 – under 11·0** includes times from 10·5 seconds to just under 11·0 seconds.

Class intervals	Tally marks	Frequency
10·5 – under 11·0		
11·0 – under 11·5		
11·5 – under 12·0		
12·0 – under 12·5		
12·5 – under 13·0		
13·0 – under 13·5		

2 (a) Copy and complete the frequency table for the 100-metres sprint.
  (b) Copy and complete this bar graph to show the information in your frequency table.

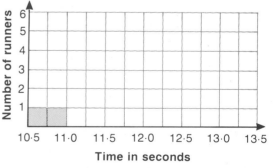

3 Here are the results from two other events. For each event
  (a) choose suitable class intervals and draw a frequency table
  (b) draw a bar graph of the results.

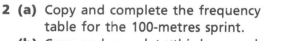

Javelin distance in metres				
52·7	53·4	52·1	53·6	54·2
52·5	53·7	52·6	53·8	54·0
54·6	54·9	53·0	54·1	54·5
52·9	54·1	53·5	54·0	55·1
53·5	54·0	54·2	55·0	52·9

200-metres sprint in seconds				
24·9	25·0	24·8	25·5	26·0
24·7	25·1	26·5	24·8	25·5
25·1	26·4	25·9	24·8	26·0
26·2	25·8	25·5	26·5	24·5
24·6	25·0	25·9	26·1	25·0

The geography class is going on an outing and Mr James, the school cook, has to prepare the packed lunches. Mr James would like to know:
- who is going, and their choice of packed lunch
- how many of each item of food and drink he will need
- whether the same items are equally popular with boys and girls.

Work in a group.

1 Make up a suitable survey sheet which Mr James could use to collect the information he needs. **You** decide which items of food and drink are available.

Mr James can offer
- 4 types of sandwich .... any two
- 3 flavours of crisps .... only one
- 2 different fruits .... one only
- 4 kinds of soft drink........... one only

Each pupil can choose

2 Carry out a survey of your class using your survey sheet.

3 Organise the data from your survey and use it to
   (a) answer Mr James's questions
   (b) draw at least one graph.

4 Write about what you found in your survey.

5 A packed lunch is made up of the items most frequently chosen.
   (a) List its contents.
   (b) How many pupils chose this packed lunch?

Challenge

Ask your teacher what to do next.

To multiply by 10
move each digit
one place to the **left**.
  17·25 × 10 =
172·5 ←

To multiply by 100
move each digit
two places to the **left**.
  0·456 × 100 =
45·6 ← ←

To multiply by 1000
move each digit
three places to the **left**.
  3·567 × 1000 =
3567 ← ← ←

1 Find:

(a) 6·43 × 10   (b) 2·987 × 1000   (c) 0·847 × 10   (d) 0·315 × 1000
(e) 0·701 × 100   (f) 0·08 × 10   (g) 0·031 × 100   (h) 0·28 × 1000

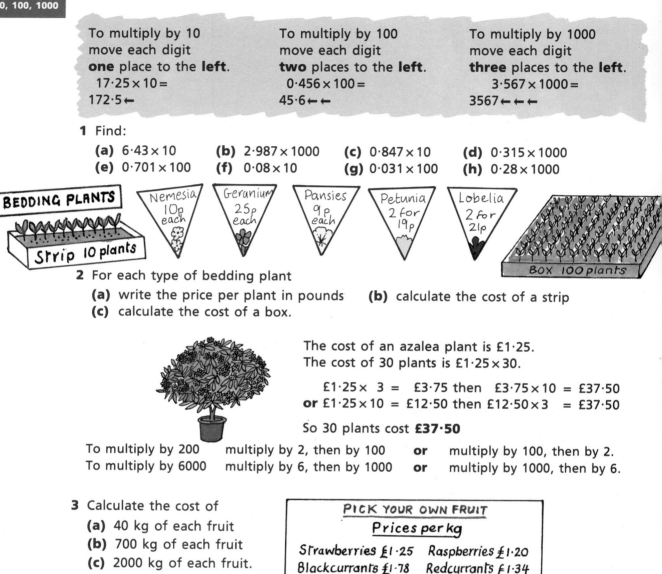

BEDDING PLANTS
Strip 10 plants

Nemesia 10p each
Geranium 25p each
Pansies 9p each
Petunia 2 for 19p
Lobelia 2 for 21p

BOX 100 plants

2 For each type of bedding plant

(a) write the price per plant in pounds   (b) calculate the cost of a strip
(c) calculate the cost of a box.

The cost of an azalea plant is £1·25.
The cost of 30 plants is £1·25 × 30.

  £1·25 × 3 = £3·75 then £3·75 × 10 = £37·50
or £1·25 × 10 = £12·50 then £12·50 × 3 = £37·50

So 30 plants cost **£37·50**

To multiply by 200   multiply by 2, then by 100   **or**   multiply by 100, then by 2.
To multiply by 6000   multiply by 6, then by 1000   **or**   multiply by 1000, then by 6.

3 Calculate the cost of

(a) 40 kg of each fruit
(b) 700 kg of each fruit
(c) 2000 kg of each fruit.

> **PICK YOUR OWN FRUIT**
> Prices per kg
>
> Strawberries £1·25   Raspberries £1·20
> Blackcurrants £1·78   Redcurrants £1·34
> Gooseberries £0·90

4 A basket of redcurrants holds an average of 1·35 kg.
What weight is in

(a) 20 baskets   (b) 300 baskets   (c) 5000 baskets?

5 How many litres of tomato fertiliser are needed to feed

(a) 50 plants   (b) 800 plants   (c) 3000 plants?

EASYGRO
Tomato Fertilizer
Use 0·475 litres per tomato plant

6 Jason dusts the earth around each tomato plant with 0·075 kg of
Pestikill powder. Calculate the weight of powder he needs for

(a) 70 plants   (b) 200 plants   (c) 4000 plants.

7 During the 10-week season Jason picked an average of 0·625 kg
of tomatoes per plant each week.

(a) What was the average weight of tomatoes per plant for the season?
(b) Calculate the total weight produced by 6000 plants for the season.

To divide by 10 move each digit **one** place to the **right**.
$243.5 \div 10 =$
→ 24.35

To divide by 100 move each digit **two** places to the **right**.
$567.8 \div 100 =$
→ → 5.678

To divide by 1000 move each digit **three** places to the **right**.
$765 \div 1000 =$
→ → 0.765

1 Find:

(a) $93.6 \div 10$ (b) $4123 \div 1000$ (c) $821.9 \div 100$ (d) $490 \div 1000$
(e) $30.9 \div 100$ (f) $4.28 \div 10$ (g) $9.8 \div 100$ (h) $0.36 \div 10$

2 Julie cut a 235 cm length of twine into 10 equal pieces. How long was each piece?

3 Julie pots plants in compost. Find the average weight of compost per plant in kg

(a) 1000 geraniums need 375 kg
(b) 100 fuchsias need 29 kg.

4 The 10 staff in the Sandydale Café share their tips equally. One weekend the total tips they collected were:

Friday £29·30   Saturday £36   Sunday £19·50.

For each day calculate one person's share of the tips.

The cost of 30 plant holders is £124·50.
The cost of one is £124·50 ÷ 30.

$£124.50 \div 3 = £41.50$ then $£41.50 \div 10 = £4.15$
or $£124.50 \div 10 = £12.45$ then $£12.45 \div 3 = £4.15$

So one plant holder costs **£4·15**

To divide by 200   divide by 2, then by 100   **or** divide by 100, then by 2.
To divide by 6000   divide by 6, then by 1000   **or** divide by 1000, then by 6.

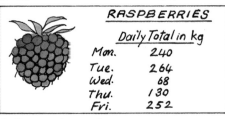

RASPBERRIES	
Daily Total in kg	
Mon.	240
Tue.	264
Wed.	68
Thu.	130
Fri.	252

5 The table shows the weights of raspberries picked by 20 teenagers. For each day calculate the average weight of raspberries per person.

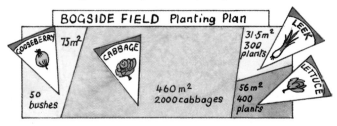

BOGSIDE FIELD Planting Plan

GOOSEBERRY 75m² 50 bushes

CABBAGE 460 m² 2000 cabbages

LEEK 31·5m² 300 plants

LETTUCE 56 m² 400 plants

6 For each section of the field find the area of ground in m² per plant.

7 Seventy-five tonnes of peat are put into 3000 bags. Find the average weight of peat per bag   (a) in tonnes   (b) in kg.

8 Last year Sandydale opened 6 days per week for 50 weeks. It made a total profit of £57 342. Calculate the average profit per working day.

On Sandydale Farm Ammon planted out 1300 strawberry plants in 28 rows.
To the nearest whole number what is the mean, or average, number of plants per row?

Enter `1300.` Press `÷` `2` `8` `=` to give `46.428571`

46·428 571 is between 46 and 47.
It is nearer 46.
The mean number of plants per row is **46 to the nearest whole number**.

46·428 571

46·4

46   47

1 For each fruit find to the nearest whole number
the mean number of plants per row.

	Strawberries	Raspberries	Gooseberries	Blackcurrants	Redcurrants
Number of plants	1400	2600	1550	2060	2000
Number of rows	26	49	42	32	36

Ammon picked 36·9 kg of fruit in 7 days. **To the first decimal place** what was the mean, or average, weight of fruit he picked per day in kg?

Enter `36.9` Press `÷` `7` `=` to give `5.2714285`

5·271 428 5 is between 5·2 and 5·3.
It is nearer 5·3.
The mean weight of fruit picked per day was **5·3 kg to the first decimal place.**

5·271 428 5

5.27

5·2   5·3

2 For each person in the table find
to the first decimal place the
mean weight of fruit picked per
day in kg.

	Paula	Jaira	Theo	Vera
Weight of fruit in kg	19·3	36·9	45·2	45·5
Number of days	3	8	7	9

3 Jackie, Awaz, Alan and Fiona spent 7 days at the farm picking fruit.
For each person, find

(a) **to the first decimal place**
the mean weight of
strawberries per basket in kg

(b) the total weight of
fruit picked

(c) **to the nearest whole
number** the mean
weight of fruit picked
per day in kg.

	Strawberries Weight	Baskets	Raspberries Weight	Gooseberries Weight
Jackie	13·8 kg	9	15·3 kg	7·5 kg
Awaz	16·7 kg	7	15·8 kg	9·4 kg
Alan	32·7 kg	12	18·1 kg	8·5 kg
Fiona	27·6 kg	14	14·9 kg	5·5 kg

Leroy picked 16·5 kg of strawberries which filled 19 baskets. **To the second decimal place** what was the average weight of strawberries per basket in kg?

Enter **16.5** Press **÷ 1 9 =** to give **0.868421**

0·868 421 is between 0·86 and 0·87.
It is nearer 0·87.
The average weight of strawberries per basket is **0·87 kg to the second decimal place.**

1 Do Workbook page 15, question 1.

2 For each person in the table calculate to the second decimal place the average weight of fruit picked per hour in kg.

Leroy		Mick		Nike	
Weight of fruit	Hours worked	Weight of fruit	Hours worked	Weight of fruit	Hours worked
89·4 kg	13	84·3 kg	14	152·3 kg	17

3 Leroy sprayed Shoo Bug on the fruit bushes. He used the quantities shown below. For each bush calculate to the second decimal place the average volume of Shoo Bug per bush in litres.

Raspberries		Gooseberries		Blackcurrants	
Shoo Bug	Bushes	Shoo Bug	Bushes	Shoo Bug	Bushes
124 litres	75	95 litres	64	140 litres	96

4 (a) The table below shows the total weight of fertiliser Leroy spread on different areas. Calculate to the second decimal place the **average** weight of fertiliser spread in **kilograms** per m² for each area of fruit.
(b) Express each average in **grams** per m².

Strawberries		Raspberries		Gooseberries	
Weight	Area	Weight	Area	Weight	Area
1·24 kg	35 m²	4·14 kg	70 m²	3·80 kg	75 m²

5 Leroy uses the tractor to spray 90 litres of liquid fertiliser on a strip of land 380 metres long in 32 minutes. Calculate to the second decimal place
(a) the average volume of fertiliser he sprayed per minute in litres
(b) the average length of strip he sprayed per minute in metres
(c) the average length of strip he sprayed per litre in metres.

Challenge

Working on Sandydale Farm

1 Use this result

$$\boxed{2}\,\boxed{3}\,\boxed{2}\;\div\;\boxed{1}\,\boxed{2}\;=\;\boxed{\textit{19.333333}}$$

to answer questions **(a)**, **(b)** and **(c)**.

(a) Angela shares 232 empty baskets
among 12 pickers.
How many baskets does she give
each picker?

(b) How many boxes each holding 12
baskets of fruit can Angela fill from
232 baskets?

(c) How many boxes each holding 12
baskets of fruit does Angela need
for 232 baskets?

2 A fully loaded tractor can carry 16 boxes of fruit. How many trips
does it need to make to carry 1461 boxes of fruit to the store?

Graham

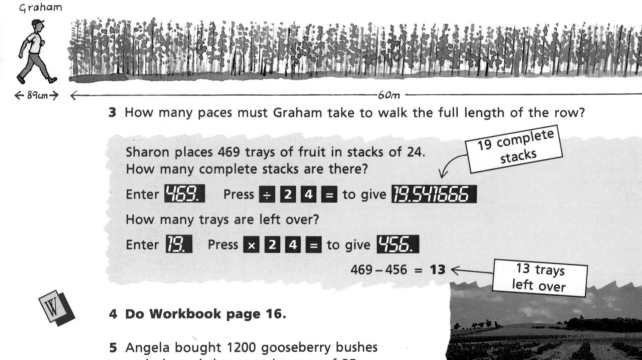

← 89cm →   ← 60m →

3 How many paces must Graham take to walk the full length of the row?

Sharon places 469 trays of fruit in stacks of 24.
How many complete stacks are there?

19 complete
stacks

Enter $\boxed{\textit{469.}}$ Press $\boxed{\div}\,\boxed{2}\,\boxed{4}\,\boxed{=}$ to give $\boxed{\textit{19.541666}}$

How many trays are left over?

Enter $\boxed{\textit{19.}}$ Press $\boxed{\times}\,\boxed{2}\,\boxed{4}\,\boxed{=}$ to give $\boxed{\textit{456.}}$

469 − 456 = **13** ← 13 trays
left over

4 Do Workbook page 16.

5 Angela bought 1200 gooseberry bushes
and planted them out in rows of 35.
How many complete rows are there?
How many bushes are left over?

6 For each kind of bush in this table, find
how many complete rows there are and
the number of bushes left over.

	Raspberries	Blackberries	Redcurrants	Loganberries
Number of bushes bought	6200	7900	13 300	15 500
Number planted in each row	47	53	59	62

Ask your teacher what to do next.

You need square dot paper.

Some of the most beautiful buildings in the world are decorated with Islamic patterns.

1 Draw an Islamic pattern using the instructions below.

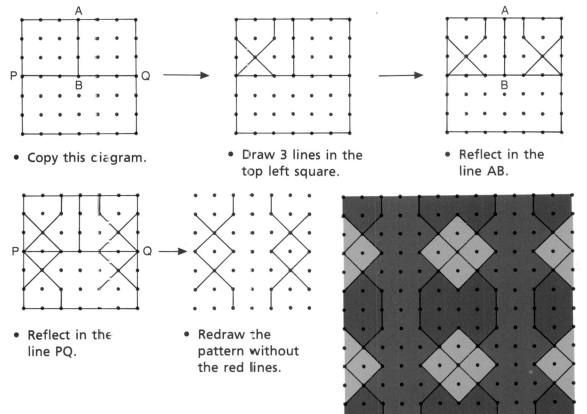

- Copy this diagram.

- Draw 3 lines in the top left square.

- Reflect in the line AB.

- Reflect in the line PQ.

- Redraw the pattern without the red lines.

- Extend and colour the pattern.

2 Repeat the instructions to draw an Islamic pattern from each of the following.

(a)   **(b)**   **(c)**   **(d)**

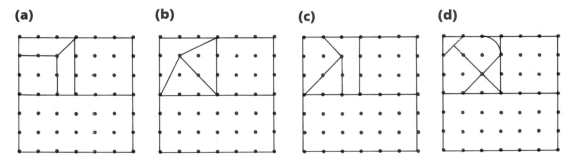

3 Repeat the instructions to draw your own Islamic pattern starting in the top left square with
  (a) 3 lines   **(b)** 4 lines.

Ask your teacher what to do next.

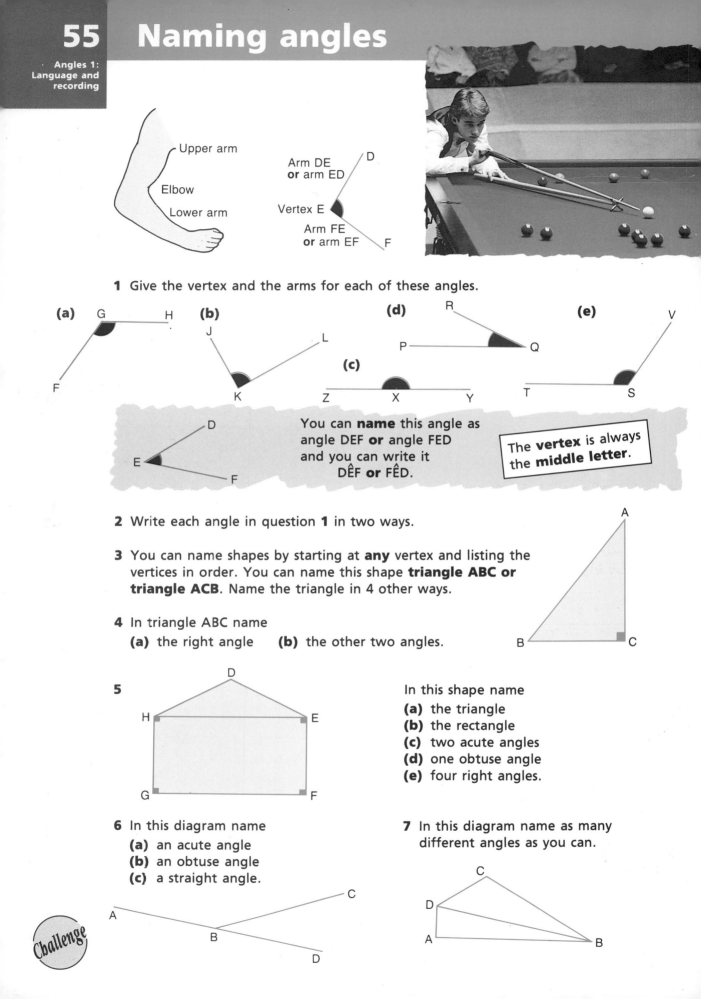

Upper arm

Elbow

Lower arm

Arm DE
or arm ED

Vertex E

Arm FE
or arm EF

1 Give the vertex and the arms for each of these angles.

(a) **(b)** **(d)** **(e)**

(c)

You can **name** this angle as
angle DEF **or** angle FED
and you can write it
DÊF **or** FÊD.

The **vertex** is always
the **middle letter**.

2 Write each angle in question **1** in two ways.

3 You can name shapes by starting at **any** vertex and listing the
vertices in order. You can name this shape **triangle ABC or
triangle ACB**. Name the triangle in 4 other ways.

4 In triangle ABC name
  (a) the right angle   **(b)** the other two angles.

5

In this shape name
  (a) the triangle
  (b) the rectangle
  (c) two acute angles
  (d) one obtuse angle
  (e) four right angles.

6 In this diagram name
  (a) an acute angle
  (b) an obtuse angle
  (c) a straight angle.

7 In this diagram name as many
different angles as you can.

Challenge

1 (a) What type of angle is RŜT?
(b) Estimate its size in degrees.

2 This flowchart gives
instructions to **measure** RŜT.

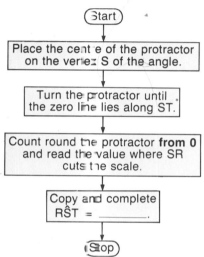

Start

Place the centre of the protractor
on the vertex S of the angle.

Turn the protractor until
the zero line lies along ST.

Count round the protractor **from 0**
and read the value where SR
cuts the scale.

Copy and complete
RŜT = _____ .

Stop

3 Explain why RŜT does **not** equal 63°.

4 Do Workbook page 17, question 1.

5 This flowchart gives instructions
for **drawing** angle **ABC = 63°**.

Start

Draw line BC 6 cm long.

Place the protractor at B as
shown. Mark 63°.

Label the mark A. Join AB.

Stop

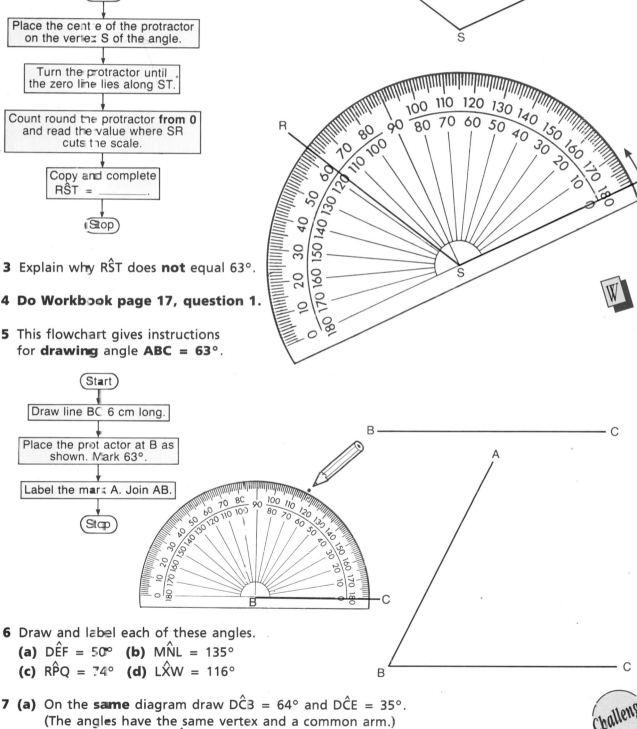

6 Draw and label each of these angles.
(a) DÊF = 50° **(b)** MN̂L = 135°
(c) RP̂Q = 74° **(d)** LX̂W = 116°

7 (a) On the **same** diagram draw DĈB = 64° and DĈE = 35°.
(The angles have the same vertex and a common arm.)
(b) What is the size of BĈE in your drawing?

Challenge

1 From Isle Bay what lies to the
   (a) North   **(b)** West
   (c) South   **(d)** North West
   (e) South West   **(f)** South East?

2 From Windy Hill what lies to the
   (a) East   **(b)** West
   (c) North West   **(d)** North East?

3 What is the direction of
   (a) Windy Pier from the castle
   (b) Windy Hill from the castle
   (c) the castle from Windy Hill
   (d) the jetty from Green Point
   (e) Green Point from the jetty
   (f) Green Point from Grey Beach?

4 George runs a ferry boat from the jetty. He sailed East until
he reached land and then set off South West. What was the
next place he reached?

5 What is the size in degrees of the angle between
   (a) N and E   **(b)** S and SW   **(c)** W and N
   (d) NE and SW   **(e)** N and SE   **(f)** N and SW?

Angles used in giving directions are called bearings.
Three-figure bearings are measured **clockwise** from **North**.
The bearing of North is 000°, East is 090°, North West is 315°.

Bearing 315°

6 Write these directions as bearings.
(a) N   **(b)** S   **(c)** E   **(d)** W   **(e)** NE   **(f)** SW

7 From Isle Bay give the bearing of
   (a) Windy Pier   **(b)** the castle   **(c)** Windy Hill
   (d) the Pine forest   **(e)** Green Point   **(f)** the jetty.

8 What lies on a bearing of
   (a) 180° from Green Point
   (b) 315° from Green Point
   (c) 045° from Windy Pier
   (d) 225° from the jetty
   (e) 045° from Windy Hill
   (f) 090° from Windy Pier?

9 Jenny left the boat house and sailed to Green Point,
then to Grey Beach, the jetty and Isle Bay. Copy and
complete her entry in the log book.

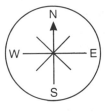

Sailed from
the Boathouse
on a bearing
of 270° for
Green Point
then changed
course to
....
and sailed

to Grey
Beach, then
....

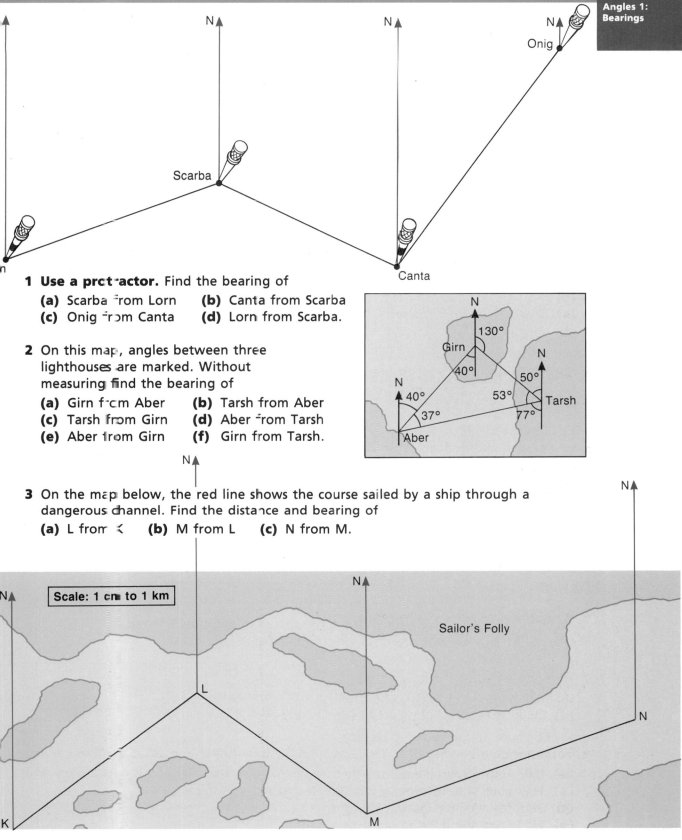

1 **Use a protractor.** Find the bearing of
   (a) Scarba from Lorn   **(b)** Canta from Scarba
   (c) Onig from Canta   **(d)** Lorn from Scarba.

2 On this map, angles between three
   lighthouses are marked. Without
   measuring find the bearing of
   (a) Girn from Aber   **(b)** Tarsh from Aber
   (c) Tarsh from Girn   **(d)** Aber from Tarsh
   (e) Aber from Girn   **(f)** Girn from Tarsh.

3 On the map below, the red line shows the course sailed by a ship through a
   dangerous channel. Find the distance and bearing of
   (a) L from K   **(b)** M from L   **(c)** N from M.

Scale: 1 cm to 1 km

4 What would be the bearings on the return journey through the channel?

5 **Do Workbook page 17, question 3.**

Paul, Mike and Theo have won the Star Prize of a Greek island cruise.
Before leaving they each set their video recorders to record their favourite TV
programmes.

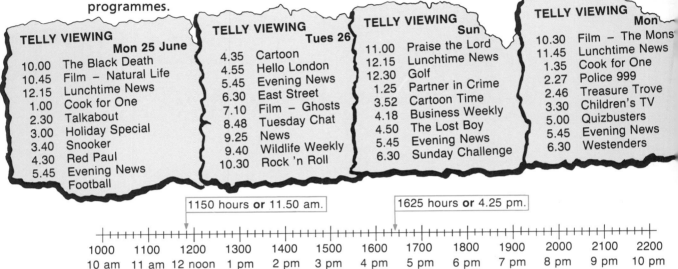

**TELLY VIEWING
Mon 25 June**

10.00 The Black Death
10.45 Film – Natural Life
12.15 Lunchtime News
1.00 Cook for One
2.30 Talkabout
3.00 Holiday Special
3.40 Snooker
4.30 Red Paul
5.45 Evening News
Football

**TELLY VIEWING
Tues 26**

4.35 Cartoon
4.55 Hello London
5.45 Evening News
6.30 East Street
7.10 Film – Ghosts
8.48 Tuesday Chat
9.25 News
9.40 Wildlife Weekly
10.30 Rock 'n Roll

**TELLY VIEWING
Sun**

11.00 Praise the Lord
12.15 Lunchtime News
12.30 Golf
1.25 Partner in Crime
3.52 Cartoon Time
4.18 Business Weekly
4.50 The Lost Boy
5.45 Evening News
6.30 Sunday Challenge

**TELLY VIEWING
Mon**

10.30 Film – The Mons
11.45 Lunchtime News
1.35 Cook for One
2.27 Police 999
2.46 Treasure Trove
3.30 Children's TV
5.00 Quizbusters
5.45 Evening News
6.30 Westenders

| 1150 hours **or** 11.50 am. | | 1625 hours **or** 4.25 pm. |

| 1000 | 1100 | 1200 | 1300 | 1400 | 1500 | 1600 | 1700 | 1800 | 1900 | 2000 | 2100 | 2200 |
| 10 am | 11 am | 12 noon | 1 pm | 2 pm | 3 pm | 4 pm | 5 pm | 6 pm | 7 pm | 8 pm | 9 pm | 10 pm |

1 The video recorders use 24-hour clocks.
Copy and complete the table **using 24-hour times**.

	Programme	Date	Start time	Finish time
Paul	The Black Death			1045
	East Street		1830	
	Quizbusters			
Mike	Talkabout			
	Golf			1325
	The Monster			
Theo	Snooker			
	Ghosts			
		26 June		2230

2 (a) Calculate how long each of the programmes in question **1** lasted.
(b) Which boy **cannot** record all his programmes on a 3-hour
tape? Explain your answer.

Mike, Paul and Theo are flying to Venice
to join the cruise ship. Paul's father is
going to drive them to the airport. The
planned route and expected travelling
times are shown.

3 (a) Calculate the total expected
travelling time to the airport.
(b) The boys want to be at the airport
by 11 pm. What is the latest time
that Paul's dad should leave his house?

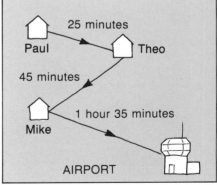

4 (a) They actually leave **Mike's** house at 9.06 pm. At what time
should they arrive at the airport?
(b) How many minutes would they have to spare?

INTERNATIONAL DEPARTURES		
FLIGHT	**DESTINATION**	**TIME**
....	Palma	2205
....	Nice	2230
....	Minorca	2240
....	New York	2320
....	Amsterdam	2345
....	Moscow	0010
....	Paris	0055
....	Venice	0120
....	Faro	0210

Our flight leaves at 0120 hours.

That's twenty past one in the morning.

Or 1.20 am

1 Write the times of the other flights in
   (a) words   **(b)** 12-hour time.

2 All flights were delayed by **90 minutes**. The flight to Minorca
should have left at 2240.

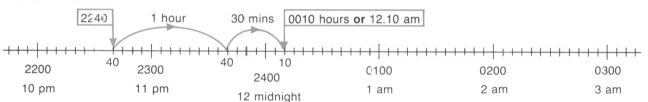

2240   1 hour   30 mins   0010 hours **or** 12.10 am

2200   40   2300   40   10   2400   0100   0200   0300
10 pm   11 pm   12 midnight   1 am   2 am   3 am

So the flight to Minorca left at **0010 hours** or **12.10 am**.

Write the new times of the other flights in the
same way.

The boys joined the cruise ship in time for breakfast.

3 Write in **12-hour time** when the ship
   (a) leaves Venice
   (b) arrives in Rhodes
   (c) arrives in Dubrovnik.

4 On which day does the ship stay at sea?

5 Calculate the number of hours
   spent in port at
   (a) Piraeus   **(b)** Crete.

CRUISE TIMETABLE			
DAY	**PORT**	**ARRIVAL**	**DEPARTURE**
Day 1	Venice		1100
Day 2	At sea through Corinth Canal		
Day 3	Piraeus	1100	2100
Day 4	Rhodes	1400	2000
Day 5	Crete	0700	1200
Day 6	Corfu	1400	1900
Day 7	Dubrovnik	0700	1200
Day 8	Venice	0900	Disembarkation after breakfast

How long are we at sea
between Rhodes and Crete?

2000 hours to midnight is 4 hours and 7 hours
more – that makes 11 hours altogether.

6 How long is spent at sea between
   (a) Corfu and Dubrovnik   **(b)** Crete and Corfu   **(c)** Venice and Piraeus?

7 Calculate the **total** length of time spent **at sea** during the cruise.

While in Corfu, Paul, Mike and Theo entered the jet-ski race.

JET·SKI RACE
3 trial laps
then
4 lap race
Fastest time wins
MEAL FOR 2

Paul's trial times were:

Lap 1	56 seconds
Lap 2	52 seconds
Lap 3	49 seconds
Total time	157 seconds = **2 minutes 37 seconds**

60 seconds = 1 minute
120 seconds = 2 minutes
180 seconds = 3 minutes

1 Change these times to minutes and seconds.

(a) 70 seconds **(b)** 95 seconds **(c)** 163 seconds **(d)** 178 seconds
(e) 200 seconds **(f)** 193 seconds **(g)** 240 seconds **(h)** 345 seconds

2 Here are Mike's and Theo's times in seconds for their trial laps.

	Mike	Theo
Lap 1	59 s	52 s
Lap 2	55 s	58 s
Lap 3	52 s	45 s

Find their total times in minutes and seconds.

In the race each lap is timed **to the nearest hundredth (0·01) of a second**. Paul's lap times are:

Lap 1	54·89 s
Lap 2	51·45 s
Lap 3	57·04 s
Lap 4	52·55 s
Total time	215·93 s = **3 minutes 35·93 seconds**

180 seconds = 3 minutes
215 seconds = 3 minutes 35 seconds

3 Here are the times in seconds for the other racers.

	Mike	Theo	Linda	Monica
Lap 1	53·66	49·44	56·19	48·92
Lap 2	48·33	54·92	51·10	51·15
Lap 3	53·72	48·86	57·25	47·93
Lap 4	56·61	49·46	49·90	54·61

(a) Find each racer's total time in minutes and seconds.
(b) Who won the meal?

**Time:
Practical
measurement**

Work with a partner.

One of you should attempt the tasks from Section 1
and the other those from Section 2.
Your partner times and checks each task you do.
Add a 5-second penalty for each mistake.
Fill in your times for each task on **Workbook page 18**.

Section 1

Task 1   Copy out this passage.

The largest living land animal is the African bush elephant
(*Loxodonta africana*). The average bull elephant stands
3·2 metres (10 ft 6 in) at the shoulder and weighs 5·7 tonnes
(5·6 tons). The largest specimen ever recorded was a bull shot
in Southern Angola in 1974. This elephant was 4·16 metres
(13 ft 8 in) tall and weighed 12·2 tonnes (12 tons).

Task 2   Use the grid on **Workbook page 18**
for the number puzzle.

Across		Down	
1	11×12	**1**	13 squared
3	$9 \times 9 + 10$	**2**	$4 \times 8 - 3$
5	$105 - 9$	**4**	12 dozen
7	51×4	**6**	$37 + 29 - 4$

Task 3   Do the pencil race on **Workbook page 18**.

Section 2

Task 1   Copy out this passage.

The largest wild mammal in the British Isles is the red deer
(*Cervus elaphus*). A full-grown stag stands 1·11 metres
(3 ft 8 in) at the shoulder and weighs 109 kg (240 lb). The
heaviest specimen ever recorded was a stag killed at
Glenfiddich, Scotland in 1831. The stag was 1·37 metres
(4 ft 6 in) tall and weighed 238 kg (525 lb).

Task 2   Use the grid on **Workbook page 18**
for the number puzzle.

Across		Down	
1	13 dozen	**1**	11 squared
3	$8 \times 7 - 4$	**2**	$9 \times 8 - 7$
5	$12 + 15 - 11$	**4**	54×4
7	18×7	**6**	$80 - 19$

Task 3   Do the pencil race on **Workbook page 18**.

Ask your teacher what to do next.

Did you know?
• In summer the Forth
  Bridge is about 1 m
  longer than in winter
  because the metal expands.
• About 6 500 000 rivets
  (total weight 4200 tonnes)
  were used in the bridge.

1 Do Workbook page 19.

2 The photograph above shows structures with triangular
sections. These structures are all strong and **rigid.**

Work as a group. You need strips and fasteners.

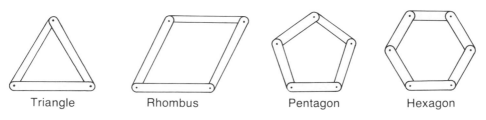

Triangle   Rhombus   Pentagon   Hexagon

(a) Make each of these frameworks with strips.
(b) Try to push each framework out of shape without breaking
the strips. A framework which cannot easily be pushed
out of shape is **rigid**. Which of these frameworks is rigid?
(c) A framework can often be made rigid by adding
diagonal strips to make triangles. Add **two** diagonal
strips like this to the pentagon.
Is the framework rigid now?
(d) In the same way, make the rhombus and the hexagon
rigid.
(e) Copy this table and enter your results.

Number of sides	3	4	5	6	7	8	9	10
Number of diagonal strips to make the shape rigid	0		2					

(f) From the pattern of numbers, complete the table.

3 Use the pattern in the table to find how many diagonal strips
are needed to make rigid a framework with
(a) 20 sides   **(b)** 100 sides.

4 (a) Look for triangles in the rigid structures shown.
(b) Name other objects in which triangles are used for
rigidity.

Ask your teacher what to do next.

25% OFF VIDEO

10% OFF

½%* COMMISSION

PERSONAL HI-FI 50% OFF

20% OFF TVs

25% MORE CUSTARD THAN a 425 g CAN

PLUS 10%

12% EXTRA FREE AT MRP 18p

1 Use newspapers and magazines. Cut out and display examples of percentages.

23% means: ↗ 23 out of 100 ↘ $\frac{23}{100}$

65% means: ↗ 65 out of 100 ↘ $\frac{65}{100}$

2 Each flag is divided into 100 equal parts. Find the percentage coloured red, blue and green.
Write your answers like this:

(a) Red $\frac{51}{100}$ = 51%

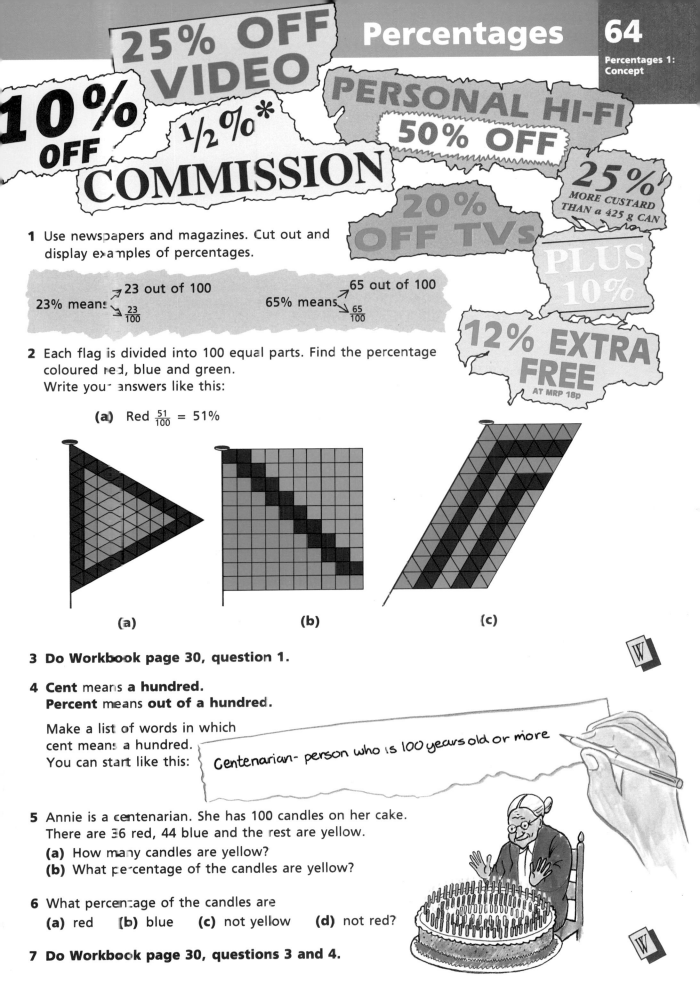

(a)　　　　　　　(b)　　　　　　　(c)

3 Do Workbook page 30, question 1.

4 Cent means **a hundred.**
Percent means **out of a hundred.**

Make a list of words in which cent means a hundred.
You can start like this:

Centenarian- person who is 100 years old or more

5 Annie is a centenarian. She has 100 candles on her cake.
There are 36 red, 44 blue and the rest are yellow.

(a) How many candles are yellow?
(b) What percentage of the candles are yellow?

6 What percentage of the candles are

(a) red　　**(b)** blue　　**(c)** not yellow　　**(d)** not red?

7 Do Workbook page 30, questions 3 and 4.

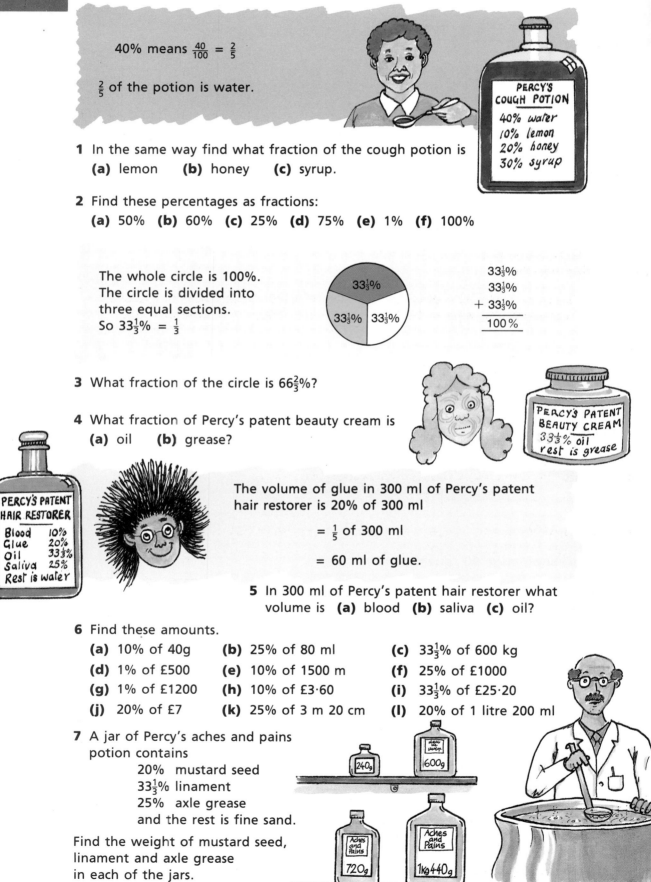

40% means $\frac{40}{100} = \frac{2}{5}$

$\frac{2}{5}$ of the potion is water.

PERCY'S COUGH POTION
40% water
10% lemon
20% honey
30% syrup

1 In the same way find what fraction of the cough potion is
  (a) lemon   **(b)** honey   **(c)** syrup.

2 Find these percentages as fractions:
  (a) 50% **(b)** 60% **(c)** 25% **(d)** 75% **(e)** 1% **(f)** 100%

The whole circle is 100%.
The circle is divided into
three equal sections.
So $33\frac{1}{3}\% = \frac{1}{3}$

$33\frac{1}{3}\%$
$33\frac{1}{3}\%$
$+ \ 33\frac{1}{3}\%$
_____
100%

3 What fraction of the circle is $66\frac{2}{3}\%$?

4 What fraction of Percy's patent beauty cream is
  (a) oil   **(b)** grease?

PERCY'S PATENT BEAUTY CREAM
$33\frac{1}{3}\%$ oil
rest is grease

PERCY'S PATENT HAIR RESTORER

Blood   10%
Glue   20%
Oil $33\frac{1}{3}\%$
Saliva   25%
Rest is water

The volume of glue in 300 ml of Percy's patent
hair restorer is 20% of 300 ml

$= \frac{1}{5}$ of 300 ml

$= 60$ ml of glue.

5 In 300 ml of Percy's patent hair restorer what
  volume is **(a)** blood **(b)** saliva **(c)** oil?

6 Find these amounts.
  (a) 10% of 40g   **(b)** 25% of 80 ml   **(c)** $33\frac{1}{3}\%$ of 600 kg
  (d) 1% of £500   **(e)** 10% of 1500 m   **(f)** 25% of £1000
  (g) 1% of £1200   **(h)** 10% of £3·60   **(i)** $33\frac{1}{3}\%$ of £25·20
  (j) 20% of £7   **(k)** 25% of 3 m 20 cm   **(l)** 20% of 1 litre 200 ml

7 A jar of Percy's aches and pains
  potion contains
         20% mustard seed
         $33\frac{1}{3}\%$ linament
         25% axle grease
         and the rest is fine sand.

Find the weight of mustard seed,
linament and axle grease
in each of the jars.

240g   600g

720g   1kg 440g

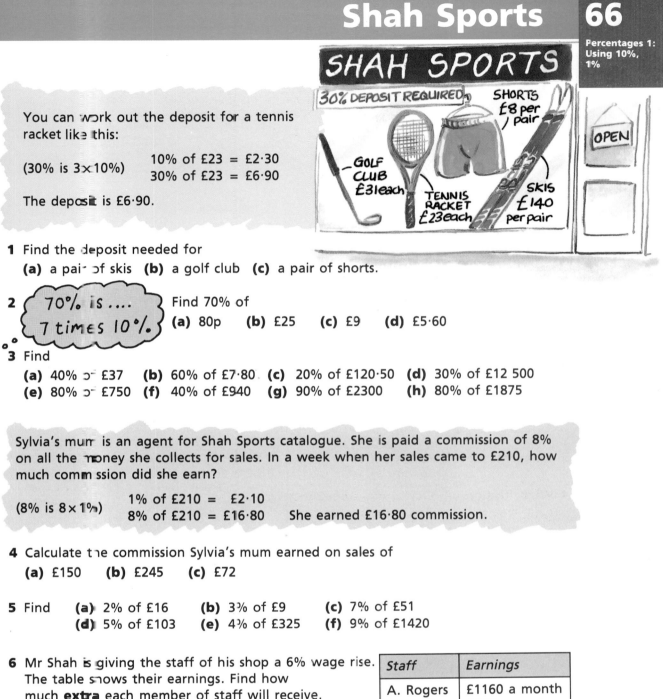

You can work out the deposit for a tennis racket like this:

(30% is 3×10%)

10% of £23 = £2·30
30% of £23 = £6·90

The deposit is £6·90.

1 Find the deposit needed for
   (a) a pair of skis **(b)** a golf club **(c)** a pair of shorts.

2 70% is ....
   7 times 10%.

Find 70% of
   (a) 80p   **(b)** £25   **(c)** £9   **(d)** £5·60

3 Find
   (a) 40% of £37   **(b)** 60% of £7·80   **(c)** 20% of £120·50   **(d)** 30% of £12 500
   (e) 80% of £750   **(f)** 40% of £940   **(g)** 90% of £2300   **(h)** 80% of £1875

Sylvia's mum is an agent for Shah Sports catalogue. She is paid a commission of 8% on all the money she collects for sales. In a week when her sales came to £210, how much commission did she earn?

(8% is 8×1%)

1% of £210 = £2·10
8% of £210 = £16·80   She earned £16·80 commission.

4 Calculate the commission Sylvia's mum earned on sales of
   (a) £150   **(b)** £245   **(c)** £72

5 Find   **(a)** 2% of £16   **(b)** 3% of £9   **(c)** 7% of £51
            (d) 5% of £103   **(e)** 4% of £325   **(f)** 9% of £1420

6 Mr Shah is giving the staff of his shop a 6% wage rise. The table shows their earnings. Find how much **extra** each member of staff will receive.

Staff	Earnings
A. Rogers	£1160 a month
W. Archer	£115 a week
S. Coia	£16 a day
F. Reid	£3 an hour

Shah Sports shop sells 'high energy' food and drinks.

7 For a 400 g packet of Carbocose, calculate the weight of
   (a) fibre, 20%   **(b)** carbohydrate, 70%
   (c) protein, 6%   **(d)** fat, 4%.

8 For a 570 ml bottle of Glucplan, calculate the volume of
   (a) minerals, 1%   **(b)** protein, 3%
   (c) fat, 6%   **(d)** water, 90%.

Ask your teacher what to do next.

This is a plan of Celie's front garden.
It is **not** an accurate scale diagram.

Follow the steps to make
accurate scale drawings
of the triangles.

Use a scale of **1 cm to 1 m**.

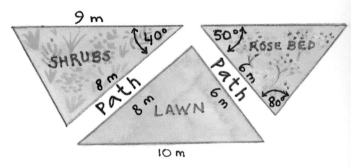

1 In the **lawn** triangle Celie knows the lengths of the **three sides.**
Use a ruler and compasses.

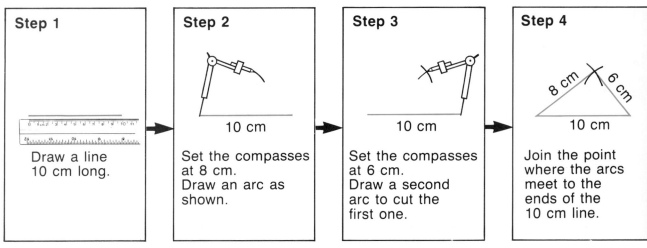

Step 1	Step 2	Step 3	Step 4
Draw a line 10 cm long.	Set the compasses at 8 cm. Draw an arc as shown.	Set the compasses at 6 cm. Draw a second arc to cut the first one.	Join the point where the arcs meet to the ends of the 10 cm line.

This completes the **lawn** triangle.

2 In the **shrubs** triangle Celie knows **one angle** and the lengths of **two sides**.
Use a ruler and a protractor.

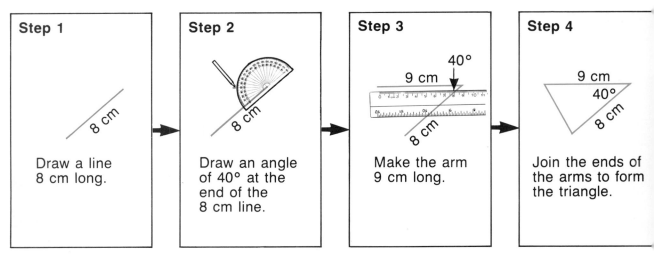

Step 1	Step 2	Step 3	Step 4
Draw a line 8 cm long.	Draw an angle of 40° at the end of the 8 cm line.	Make the arm 9 cm long.	Join the ends of the arms to form the triangle.

This completes the **shrubs** triangle.

3 In the **rose bed** triangle Celie knows **two angles** and the length of **one side**.
Use a ruler and a protractor to draw it.

Celie is planning some more lawns and flower beds.

Draw accurate full-size drawings of these triangles for Celie.
The lengths are in centimetres.

1 Draw these like the **lawn** triangle.

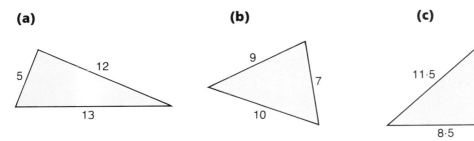

(a)   **(b)**   **(c)**

2 Draw these like the **shrubs** triangle.

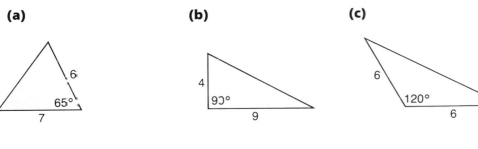

(a)   **(b)**   **(c)**

3 Draw these like the **rose bed** triangle.

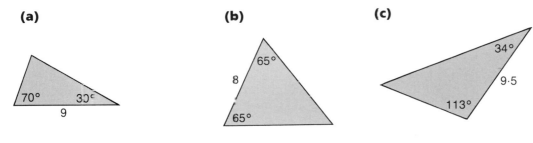

(a)   **(b)**   **(c)**

4 Draw accurate full-size drawings for each of the following.

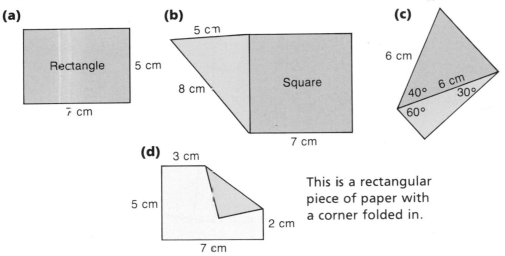

This is a rectangular
piece of paper with
a corner folded in.

The walled garden is right-angled at the corners where the gate and where the garage are.

At the corner with the tree the walls make an angle of 102°.

The garage is 6m long and 3m wide

The path is 1m wide.

The lawn and the vegetable patch are squares and come to the front wall.

The potato patch is a rectangle 2m wide.

FLOWERS

POTATOES

LAWN

VEGETABLES | GARAGE

1 Copy or trace Celie's rough plan of the garden.
Use the information above to mark sizes on your plan.

2 Use a scale of **1 cm to 1 m** to draw an accurate scale plan of the garden.

Ask your teacher what to do next.

1 Joe makes 4 cm bolts using the −4 machine. He feeds different lengths of steel bars into the machine. It cuts 4 cm from each bar and the remainder comes out on the conveyor belt. Copy and complete the table.

Length IN in cm		Length OUT in cm
	→ −4 →	
15	→ −4 →	11
16	→ −4 →	
14	→ −4 →	
	→ −4 →	13
	→ −4 →	14

2 Joyce works out the wages. The rate of pay is £5 per hour. She uses her calculator as a ×5 machine. Copy and complete the table.

Name	Number of hours		Wage in £
		→ ×5 →	
J. Burns	40	→ ×5 →	200
F. Hill	32	→ ×5 →	
A. Banks	28	→ ×5 →	
A. Imlah	39	→ ×5 →	
J. Jones		→ ×5 →	190
P. Smith		→ ×5 →	145

3 Copy and complete:

(a) 4 → ×3 → ___

(b) 8 → ÷2 → ___

(c) 23 → −7 → ___

(d) 15 → +12 → ___

(e) ___ → +8 → 21

(f) ___ → −4 → 9

(g) ___ → ÷4 → 8

(h) ___ → ×8 → 48

(i) 5 → × → 30

(j) 18 → ÷ → 6

(k) 29 → − → 14

(l) 0 → + → 10

4 Find more than one possible label (or **rule**) for each of these number machines:

(a) 4 → ? → 12   10 → ? → 5   9 → ? → 3

5 You can link machines.   2 → ×3 → 6 → +4 → 10

Copy and complete:

(a) 4 → +2 → 6 → ×3 → ___

(b) 6 → ×4 → ___ → +2 → 26

(c) 8 → ÷2 → ___ → × → 20

(d) ___ → −8 → 4 → + → 16

(e) 10 → × → 30 → ÷ → 15

(f) ___ → +4 → ___ → ×2 → 18

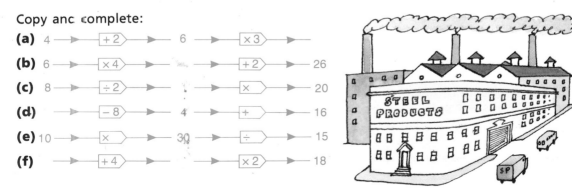

At Fareworth's the checkout staff are paid £3 per hour.

Number of hours ⟶ $\boxed{\times 3}$ ⟶ Wage, number of £

1 Use the number machine to find the wage for
   (a) Avril, 23 hours   **(b)** Tom, 40 hours   **(c)** Tania, 16 hours   **(d)** Megan, 37 hours

Number of hours ⟶ $\boxed{\times 3}$ ⟶ Wage, number of £ ⟵ You can write this as a **formula**.

$$h \times 3 = w$$ where h is the number of hours and w is the wage or number of £.

This can be written as $w = h \times 3$

You can use this formula to find Avril's wage.
She works 23 hours so **$h = 23$**.

$$w = h \times 3$$
$$w = \mathbf{23} \times 3$$
$$w = 69$$
Avril's wage is £69.

2 Copy and complete to find Tom's wage: Formula: $w = h \times 3$
when $h = \square$ $w = \square \times 3$
$$w = \square$$
Tom's wage is £ $\square$

3 Use the formula to find the wage for
   (a) Tania   **(b)** Megan   **(c)** Sheena, 29 hours   **(d)** Rose, 9·5 hours.

4 Staff at Fareworth's get a £25 Christmas bonus.

Normal wage in £ (n) ⟶ $\boxed{+ 25}$ ⟶ Chistmas wage in £ (c)

  (a) Copy and complete:
    Formula: $n + \square = \square$ where n is the normal wage in £
    $c = \boxed{}$ and c is the $\boxed{}$

  (b) Bob's normal wage is £105. $n = 105$.
    Copy and complete:
    Formula: $c = n + 25$
    when $n = \square$ $c = \square + 25$
                  $c = \square$
    Bob's Christmas wage is £ $\square$

	Bob	Arun	Beth	Chris
Normal wage in £, n	105	52	180	97

  (c) Use the formula to find the Christmas wage for each of the other staff.

5 After Christmas Fareworth's has a half-price sale.

Usual price in £ (u) ⟶ $\boxed{\div 2}$ ⟶ Sale price in £ (s)

  (a) Copy and complete:
    Formula: $u \div \square = \square$ where u is $\boxed{}$
                   and s is $\boxed{}$
    $s = \square$

USUAL PRICE £28

USUAL PRICE £68·50

  (b) Use the formula to find the sale price of these items.

4 × *a* can be shortened to 4*a*
   4 × *a* = 4*a*

7 × 3 = 3 × 7
so *r* × 3 = 3 × *r* = **3*r***

Number before letter

5*b* means **5 × *b***

1 Write in shortened form:
   (a) 7 × *b*   **(b)** 8 × *d*   **(c)** *s* × 2   **(d)** *t* × 10   **(e)** 14 × *y*

2 Write the meaning of
   (a) 6*y*   **(b)** 5*a*   **(c)** 9*z*   **(d)** 12*c*   **(e)** 20*r*

3 Copy and complete the table.

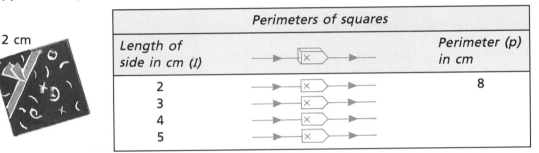

Perimeters of squares		
Length of side in cm (*l*)	→ ☐× →	Perimeter (*p*) in cm
2	→ ×☐ →	8
3	→ ×☐ →	
4	→ ×☐ →	
5	→ ×☐ →	

2 cm
2 cm

The perimeter machine is a ☐×4☐ machine.

l → ☐×4☐ → *p*

Formula: *l* × 4 = *p*   where *l* is the length of side in cm
            p = *l* × 4   and *p* is the perimeter in cm.
            p = 4 × *l*
            p = 4*l*

You can use the formula to find the perimeters of squares.

For this square *l* = 3

3 cm
3 cm

Formula: p = 4*l*
when *l* = 3   p = 4×3
                 p = 12
perimeter   = 12 cm

For a square of side 5·8 cm,
            l = 5·8
Formula: *p* = 4*l*
when *l* = 5·8 *p* = 4×5·8
                p = 23·2
perimeter   = 23·2 cm

4 Use the formula to find the perimeter of these squares:
   (a) a square of side 4 cm   **(b)** a square of side 18 cm   **(c)** a square of side 9·6 cm

Remember   An equilateral triangle
              has sides of equal length.

5 Copy and complete for an equilateral triangle:
   Formula: *l* × ☐ = *p* where *l* is ☐——————
                   and *p* is ☐——————
       p = ☐

6 Use the formula to find the perimeter of an equilateral triangle of side:
   (a) 10 cm   **(b)** 18 cm   **(c)** 7·4 cm   **(d)** 26·9 cm   **(e)** 6·25 cm

1 The number machine shows how
Mrs Green calculates the weekly
pocket money for each of her children.

Age in years (a) ⟶ ×20 ⟶ Pocket money in pence (p)

(a) Copy and complete:

Formula: $a \times \square = \square$ where a is ⬚⬚⬚⬚⬚
and p is ⬚⬚⬚⬚⬚

$\square = \square$

2 Use the formula to calculate the pocket money for:
(a) John, aged 10 years
(b) Anne, aged 8 years
(c) Mary, aged 5 years.

3 Anne is three years older than her sister Mary.

(a) Copy and complete the
number machine.

(b) Copy and complete:

Formula: $\square + \square = \square$ where ⬚⬚⬚⬚⬚
and ⬚⬚⬚⬚⬚

$\square = \square + \square$

Mary's age in years (M) ⟶ + ⟶ Anne's age in years (A)

4 Use the formula to find Anne's age when Mary is
(a) 10 years (b) 12 years (c) 21 years (d) 29 years.

5 The Greens' garden has fences
made from posts and lengths of
chain along its borders. Each fence
starts and ends with a post.

(a) Copy and complete:

Number of posts (p) ⟶ ? ⟶ Number of lengths of chain (c)

(b) Write the formula to find the
number of lengths of chain.

6 Use the formula to find the number of lengths of chain in a fence with
(a) 15 posts (b) 40 posts (c) 82 posts (d) 117 posts.

7 Mr Green works in a bike shop.
The shop sells racing bikes and mountain
bikes. Write a formula to find the **total**
number of bikes in the shop.
Use: r as the number of racing bikes
m as the number of mountain bikes
and t as the total number of bikes.

8 Use the formula to find the total
number of bikes when
(a) r is 17 and m is 20
(b) r is 9 and m is 13
(c) r is 33 and m is 26.

Ask your teacher what to do next.

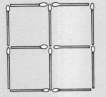

Matches

This pattern of 12 matches has five squares – four small squares and one large square.
Start with the same 12-match pattern each time.

1 Draw the pattern left when you remove:

  (a) 2 matches to leave 3 squares   **(b)** 4 matches to leave 1 square
  (c) 5 matches to leave 2 squares   **(d)** 4 matches to leave 2 squares.

2 What is the least number of matches that have to be removed
  to leave **(a)** 2 squares   **(b)** 3 squares?

Crosses

The four numbers at the ends of this cross add up to the number in the middle.

1 Find numbers to complete the crosses.

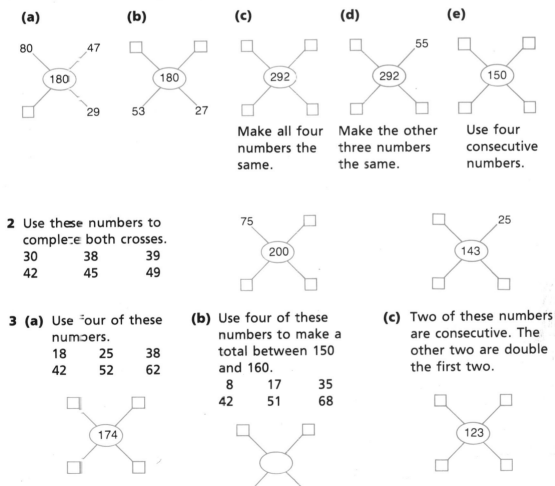

(a)

80 ⟍   47
   180
      29

(b)

□ ⟍ □
  180
53 ⟋ 27

(c)

□ ⟍ □
  292
□ ⟋ □

Make all four numbers the same.

(d)

□   55
  292
□ ⟋ □

Make the other three numbers the same.

(e)

□ ⟍ □
  150
□ ⟋ □

Use four consecutive numbers.

2 Use these numbers to complete both crosses.

  30   38   39
  42   45   49

75 ⟍ □
  200
□ ⟋ □

□   25
  143
□ ⟋ □

3 (a) Use four of these numbers.

  18   25   38
  42   52   62

□ ⟍ □
  174
□ ⟋ □

(b) Use four of these numbers to make a total between 150 and 160.

  8   17   35
  42   51   68

□ ⟍ □
  ( )
□ ⟋ □

(c) Two of these numbers are consecutive. The other two are double the first two.

□ ⟍ □
  123
□ ⟋ □

1 The number of my house
and the one next door multiply
to give 483.
What are these house numbers?

2 Two houses on the other side of the
street have numbers which multiply to
give 624.
One of these houses is directly opposite mine.
What are these house numbers?

An age-old problem

Three brothers, George, Peter and Tom,
have a total age of 39 years.

1 Write a possible age for each brother in
the first line of a table like this.

2 Use the clues to find each brother's age.
Clue 1 George, the eldest, is 11 years
older than Peter.
Clue 2 There are 4 years between
Peter and Tom.

	George	Peter	Tom
Guess 1			
Guess 2			
Guess 3			

3 In how many years will George's age
be double Peter's age?

Seeing spots

Use a die. Play this game with a partner.
- Place the die as shown so that you can see the top
  and two of the side faces. Your partner should see the
  top and the other side faces.
- Score a point if you can write the total number
  of spots your partner can see.
- Play the game several times, taking turns to
  place the die in different positions.

1 Place the die so that one of you can see nine spots
and the other eleven spots. How many spots are on the
top face?

2 In the picture John can see eleven spots and Carol seven.
How many spots are on the face resting on the table?

Hare and tortoise

A hare and a tortoise were having a race along a straight road. For some strange reason they set off in opposite directions. The hare ran at **5 metres per second** and the tortoise at **5 metres per minute**.

Make a table to find how long it took them to be 1525 metres apart.

Time in minutes	Distance hare has gone	Distance tortoise has gone	Total distance apart
1	5 × 60 = 300 m	5 × 1 = 5 m	305 m
2	5 × 60 × 2 =	5	

Dice scores

A game is played by throwing two dice, one red and the other blue.

1 List all the possible pairs of numbers in a table like this.

1, 1	1, 2	1, 3	1, 4	1, 5	1, 6
2, 1	2, 2	2, 3			
3, 1	3, 2				

2 How many possible pairs are there?

3 How many ways are there of scoring a **total** of
  (a) 12   **(b)** 9   **(c)** 7   **(d)** 3 ?

Bags of potatoes

Mr Murphy sells potatoes in 3 kg and 25 kg bags. He has 202 kg of potatoes in his van. How many bags of each weight could he have?
Make tables like these to help you.

3 kg bags		25 kg bags	
Number	Weight	Number	Weight
1	3 kg	1	25 kg
2	6 kg	2	50 kg
3	9 kg	3	

Team selection

One boy has to be chosen from **each** age group.
List all the possible teams.

ATHLETICS CLUB
Names for Sprint Team

12 years	13 years	14 years
Jim	Bill	Craig
Tom	Ahmed	Geoff
	Karim	Doug
	Eric	

Dotty picture

Anton created a pattern of
red, blue and green dots.

1 How many dots are in
each row?

2 Describe the number pattern of
(a) red dots **(b)** green dots.

	Red dots	Blue dots	Green dots
Row 1	100		
Row 2	98	2	
Row 3	96	3	1
Row 4	94	4	2
Row 5	92	5	3

3 Row 3 has 96 red dots, 3 blue dots and 1 green dot.
Describe **(a)** row 6 **(b)** row 10 **(c)** row 25 **(d)** row 50.

Dotty areas   You need centimetre square dot paper.

This shape has
- 8 dots on its boundary
- 1 dot inside
- an area of 4 cm².

1 (a) Draw at least 4 different shapes
each with only one dot inside.
(b) Copy and complete the table for
your shapes.
(c) Describe the pattern in your table.
(d) What is the area of a shape with
16 dots on its boundary and 1 dot
inside?

Number of dots on boundary	Area of shape in cm²
8	4

2 Investigate shapes with 2 dots inside.

Odd pattern

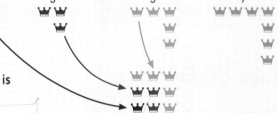

These crowns represent
odd numbers.

The sum of the **first three** odd numbers is

$1+3+5 \longrightarrow 9$ or 3^2

1 Copy and complete the table.

2 Describe the pattern in your table.

3 Use the pattern to find the sum of
(a) the **first seven** odd numbers
(b) the **first ten** odd numbers
(c) the **first twenty** odd numbers.

Sum of odd numbers	Total
1	1 or 1^2
1+3	4 or 2^2
1+3+5	9 or 3^2
1+3+5+7	
1+3+5+7+9	
1+3+5+7+9+11	

4 We describe 1+3+5 as the sum of the first three odd numbers.

Describe and find
(a) $1+3+5+7+9$
(b) $1+3+5+7+ \ldots +17+19$
(c) $1+3+5+7+ \ldots +27+29$
(d) $1+3+5+7+ \ldots +97+99$

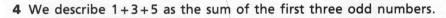

Five squares

- Colour this shape on squared paper and cut it out.

- Cut the shape into 5 squares.

- Fit the 5 squares together to make a rectangle.

- Can you fit the 5 squares together to make a 10 by 3 rectangle? Explain.

Cover up

- Copy this numbered square.

1	2	3
4	5	6
7	8	9

- Use **four** of these ☐☐ rectangles to cover **eight** of the numbered squares. Leave number 5 uncovered.

- Which other numbers could be left uncovered? What do you notice about these numbers?

Tiling rectangles

1 Copy and complete.

Rectangle	P	Q	R	S
Length in cm				
Breadth in cm				
Area in cm²				

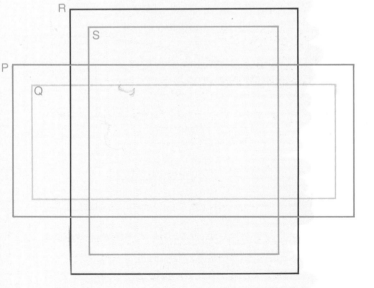

2 (a) Find the area of this tile.

(b) How many of these tiles cover each rectangle?

(c) Show on centimetre squared paper how the tiles cover each rectangle.

(d) Can you cover an 8 cm by 5 cm rectangle exactly with these tiles? Explain.

Sum of digits

Do not use the digit zero.

In each of these numbers
the sum of the digits is four.

| 121 | | 13 | | 4 |

1 (a) List all the numbers in which the sum of the digits is four.
   (b) Which of these numbers is the smallest?
   (c) Which of these numbers is the greatest?

2 Repeat question **1** for numbers in which the sum of the digits is
   (a) 2   **(b)** 3.

3 (a) Copy and complete:

Sum of digits	1	2	3	4
Number of numbers	1			

   (b) Describe the pattern in your table.
   (c) How many numbers do you think have five as the sum of the digits?
   (d) List the numbers from smallest to largest.

4 When the digit zero is used can you find the greatest number in which the sum of the digits is 5? Explain.

Windows

Annie is an architect. She designs windows
using identical panes of glass. The panes are
twice as long as they are broad.
The windows must be rectangles or squares.

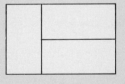

Using **1** pane, 2 window
designs are possible.

Using **2** panes, 4 window
designs are possible.

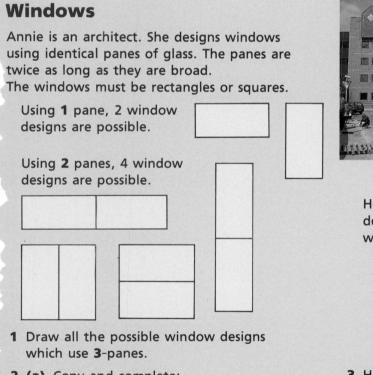

Here is one of Annie's
designs for a **3**-pane
window.

1 Draw all the possible window designs
   which use **3**-panes.

2 (a) Copy and complete:

Number of panes	1	2	3
Number of designs			

   (b) Describe the pattern in your table.

3 How many window
designs do you think
can be made using
4 panes? Check your
answer by drawing each
design.

Ask your teacher what to do next.

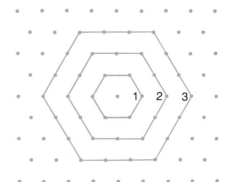

You need isometric dot paper.

1 Bimla is an architect. She has started drawing designs for a hexagonal courtyard. She wants to put posts on the perimeter of each hexagon as shown by the dots.

(a) Copy and extend Bimla's drawing until you have five hexagons.

(b) Copy and complete this table for her:

Hexagon	1	2	3	4	5
Number of posts on perimeter		12			

(c) How many posts do you think there would be on the perimeter of the next hexagon?

(d) Draw the sixth hexagon and check your answer to **(c)**.

(e) Explain how Bimla could **calculate** the number of posts on the perimeter of the tenth hexagon.

When you multiply a number by 6 the **answer** is called a **multiple of 6**.

2×6 ——→ 12

13×6 ——→ 78

29×6 ——→ 174

A multiple of 6 divides exactly by 6.

2 List all the multiples of 6 up to 60.

3 (a) Which of these numbers are multiples of 6?

96   54   120   68   42

(b) List all the multiples of 6 between 140 and 170.

4 (a) List the first ten multiples of 4.

(b) These cars are parked outside Bimla's office. Which of the numbers on their registrations are multiples of 4?

E32 KJD   G 100 FWN   D206 FYF   G224 FWN   F616 YED

You can show the multiples of 6 in a diagram like this.

Six is 0 tens and 6 units.

6 is plotted (0, 6)
12 is plotted (1, 2) and so on.

The plotted points have been joined in order.

Units

Tens

You need 1 cm squared paper.

5 Draw separate diagrams like this for

(a) the multiples of 5   **(b)** the multiples of 8   **(c)** the multiples of 7.

6 Draw a diagram for the multiples of 9. What do you notice?

John arranges 8 pennies in different rectangles like these. The table shows how he describes them.

Rectangle	Description
(2 rows of 4 pennies)	2 × 4
(1 row of 8 pennies)	1 × 8

1 He arranges **12** pennies in 3 different rectangles.
Sketch and **describe** each rectangle.

2 Sketch and describe as many different rectangles as possible for
(a) 18 pennies (b) 20 pennies (c) 24 pennies.

3 Describe all the different possible rectangles for 36 pennies.

John described the rectangles for **8** pennies as 2×4 and 1×8.
1, 2, 4 and 8 are called the **factors of 8**.

4 Use your results from questions **1**, **2** and **3** to list all the factors of
(a) 12 (b) 18 (c) 20 (d) 24 (e) 36

5 Find two numbers which each have
(a) only 3 factors (b) only 4 factors (c) only 5 factors.

6 Find six numbers which each have only 2 factors.

A number which has **only 2 factors** is called a **prime number**.

7 Which of these are prime numbers?

11 5 22 29 17

You need 1 cm squared paper.
Work with a partner.

8 Use the following method to find all the prime numbers between 1 and 36.
- Copy this 6 by 6 square.
- Cross out 1, which is **not** a prime number.
- Cross out all the multiples of 2 **except 2**.
- Cross out all the multiples of 3 **except 3**.
- Cross out all the multiples of 5 **except 5**.
- List the numbers you have left. Check that they are all prime numbers.

1	2	3	4	5	6
7	8	9	10	11	12
13	14	15	16	17	18
19	20	21	22	23	24
25	26	27	28	29	30
31	32	33	34	35	36

9 Try to find all 25 prime numbers between 1 and 100.

10 28 is a multiple of 2.
28 is the sum of two primes,
17 + 11.

Investigate whether you can write other multiples of 2 as the sum of two primes.

Did you know?

This method of finding prime numbers was worked out by a Greek mathematician called Eratosthenes who lived over 2000 years ago. It is called The Sieve of Eratosthenes.

Investigation
Investigation

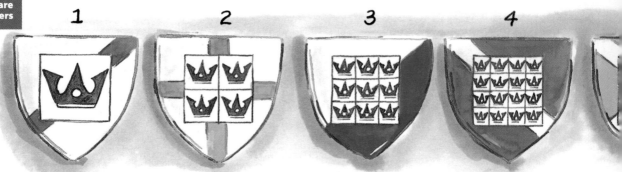

1   2   3   4

Battlefield Castle has this row of shields on display.

1 Copy and complete this table for the
Battlefield Guide Book.

Shield	1	2	3	4
Number of crowns				

2 How many crowns would there be on
  (a) the fifth shield   **(b)** the sixth shield?

3 Explain how to **calculate** the number of crowns on the tenth shield.

When a number is multipled
by itself the **answer** is called
a square number.

$4 \times 4 = 16$

16 is the square of **4**.
4×4 can be written as 4^2.
4^2 is read **4 squared**.

4 Which of these are
  square numbers?
     64   37   49   42   24   81   100

5 You can find 13^2 using your calculator. Enter **13** Press **× 1 3 =** to give **169**

Make a table like this to show the square of each number from 1 to 20.

Number	1	2	3	4	5	6	7	8	9	10	11	12	13	14	15	16	17	18	19	20
Square													169							

6 Because $169 = 13 \times 13$, **13** is called the
  square root of 169. What is the square root of

  (a) 25   **(b)** 16   **(c)** 64
  (d) 100   **(e)** 225   **(f)** 361 ?

49 is the square of 7.
 7 is the square root of 49.

7 Copy and extend each of these patterns for three more rows. Write the tenth row.

  (a) $2^2 = 4$ *How are* $3 = 1 \times 3$ **(b)** $2^2 - 1^2 = 4 - 1 = 3 = 2 + 1$
        $3^2 = 9$ ← *these →* $8 = 2 \times 4$ $3^2 - 2^2 = 9 - 4 = 5 = 3 + 2$
        $4^2 = 16$ *connected?* $15 = 3 \times 5$ $4^2 - 3^2 = 16 - 9 = 7 = 4 + 3$

8 Look at the square numbers in your table from question **5**.

$25 + 144 = 169$
So $5^2 + 12^2 = 13^2$

Find pairs of square numbers which add together to give
another square number.

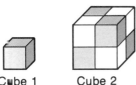
Cube 1

Cube 2

Cube 3

Cube 4

Rubik's cube was invented by a Hungarian called Ernö Rubik.

1 (a) Copy and complete this table:

(b) Explain how to **calculate** the number of small cubes in Cube 10.

Cube	1	2	3	4	5
Number of small cubes					

When you multiply a number by itself, and multiply by itself again, the **answer** is called **a cubic number**.

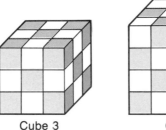
$4 \times 4 \times 4 = 64$

64 is the cube of 4.
$4 \times 4 \times 4$ can be written as 4^3.
4^3 is read **4 cubed**.

2 You can find 9^3 using your calculator.

Enter **9** Press **× 9 × 9 =** to give **729**

Make a table to show the cube of each number from 1 to 10.

3 Find the value of
(a) $3^3 + 4^3 + 5^3$ What do you notice?
(b) $1^3 + 6^3 + 8^3$ What do you notice?

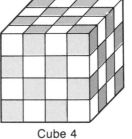
$729 = 9 \times 9 \times 9$
so 9 is called the cube root of 729.

4 Use your table to find the cube root of
(a) 8 **(b)** 125 **(c)** 512 **(d)** 343.

64 is the cube of 4.
4 is the cube root of 64.

5 Look carefully at the patterns in this table.

(a) Write the next two rows of the table.
(b) Use the pattern to find the sum of the first 10 cubic numbers.

$1^3 = \quad 1 = 1^2$	$1 = 1$
$1^3 + 2^3 = \quad 9 = 3^2$	$3 = 1 + 2$
$1^3 + 2^3 + 3^3 = \quad 36 = 6^2$	$6 = 1 + 2 + 3$
$1^3 + 2^3 + 3^3 + 4^3 = 100 = 10^2$	$10 = 1 + 2 + 3 + 4$

6 You can write the **fifth** cubic number as the sum of **five** consecutive odd numbers. Write the **third** cubic number as the sum of **three** consecutive odd numbers. Investigate other cubic numbers in this way. Write about what you find.

$125 \rightarrow 21 + 23 + 25$
$+ 27 + 29$

Investigation

Ask your teacher what to do next.

The Barton family are on holiday in Portugal. They took this graph to help them convert between Portuguese **escudos** and British **pounds**.

£2·50 converts to 600 escudos.

1 What does one small interval represent on the
  (a) pounds axis   **(b)** escudos axis?

2 Convert to escudos:
  (a) £2   **(b)** £1·50   **(c)** £3·50

3 Convert to pounds:

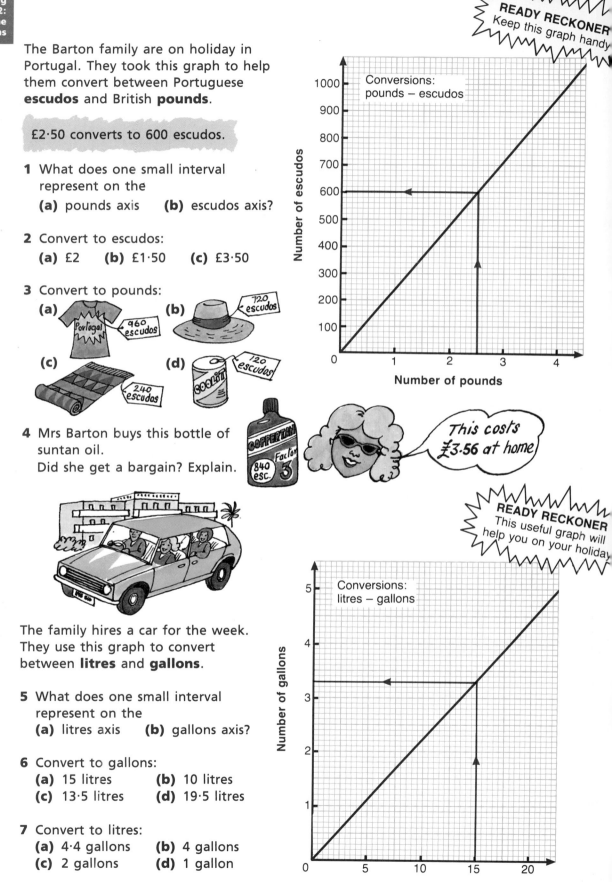

READY RECKONER
Keep this graph handy

Conversions: pounds – escudos

  (a) 960 escudos
  (b) 720 escudos
  (c) 240 escudos
  (d) 120 escudos

4 Mrs Barton buys this bottle of suntan oil.
  Did she get a bargain? Explain.

840 esc. Factor 3

This costs £3·56 at home

READY RECKONER
This useful graph will help you on your holiday

The family hires a car for the week. They use this graph to convert between **litres** and **gallons**.

5 What does one small interval represent on the
  (a) litres axis   **(b)** gallons axis?

6 Convert to gallons:
  (a) 15 litres   **(b)** 10 litres
  (c) 13·5 litres   **(d)** 19·5 litres

7 Convert to litres:
  (a) 4·4 gallons   **(b)** 4 gallons
  (c) 2 gallons   **(d)** 1 gallon

Conversions: litres – gallons

8 Do Workbook pages 31 and 32.

The graph shows the
temperatures recorded
during one day of the
Bartons' holiday.

1 What does one small
interval represent on the
  (a) temperature axis
  (b) time axis?

2 What was the temperature at
  (a) 11 am   **(b)** 4 pm
  (c) 9.24 am   **(d)** 5.36 pm?

3 What was the highest
temperature?

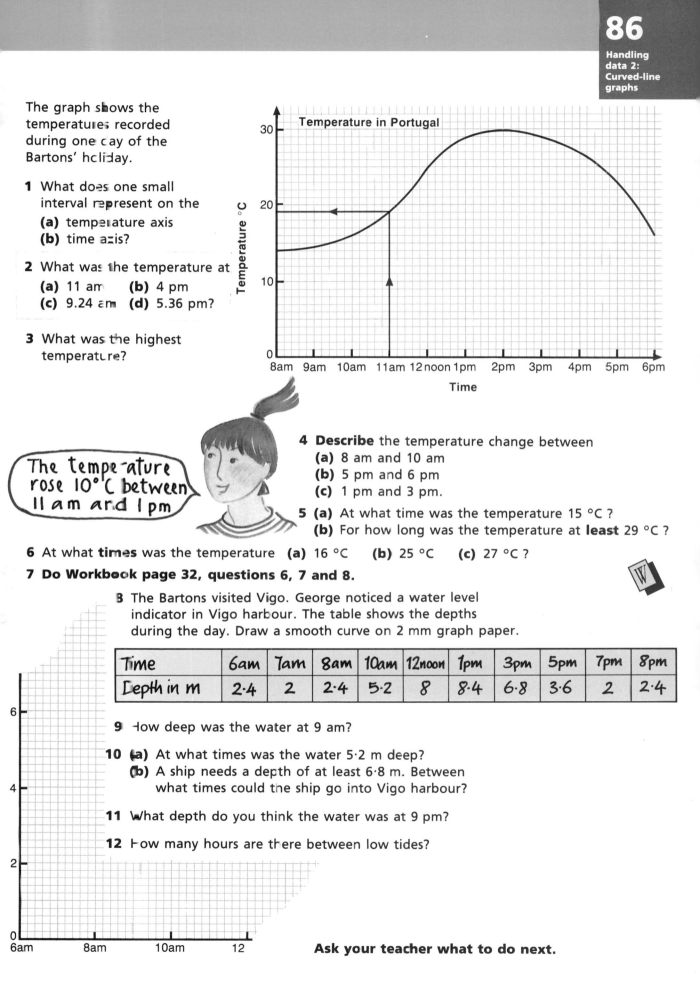

Temperature in Portugal

Temperature °C

Time

The temperature
rose 10°C between
11 am and 1 pm

4 Describe the temperature change between
  (a) 8 am and 10 am
  (b) 5 pm and 6 pm
  (c) 1 pm and 3 pm.

5 (a) At what time was the temperature 15 °C ?
  (b) For how long was the temperature at **least** 29 °C ?

6 At what **times** was the temperature **(a)** 16 °C   **(b)** 25 °C   **(c)** 27 °C ?

7 Do Workbook page 32, questions 6, 7 and 8.

8 The Bartons visited Vigo. George noticed a water level
indicator in Vigo harbour. The table shows the depths
during the day. Draw a smooth curve on 2 mm graph paper.

Time	6am	7am	8am	10am	12noon	1pm	3pm	5pm	7pm	8pm
Depth in m	2·4	2	2·4	5·2	8	8·4	6·8	3·6	2	2·4

9 How deep was the water at 9 am?

10 (a) At what times was the water 5·2 m deep?
  (b) A ship needs a depth of at least 6·8 m. Between
         what times could the ship go into Vigo harbour?

11 What depth do you think the water was at 9 pm?

12 How many hours are there between low tides?

Ask your teacher what to do next.

This road network has 3 junctions each marked
by a red dot.
Ismael drew the network using the following rules.

Rules
- Draw a continuous line.
- Do not go along any line
  more than once.
- You may pass through a
  junction more than once.

Here is Ismael's drawing of the network.

1 Which of these networks can you draw using the rules?

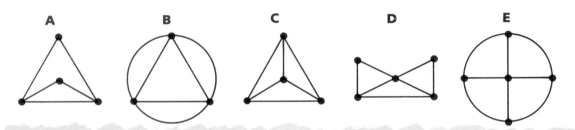

Ismael sorted the junctions into **odd** junctions and **even** junctions.

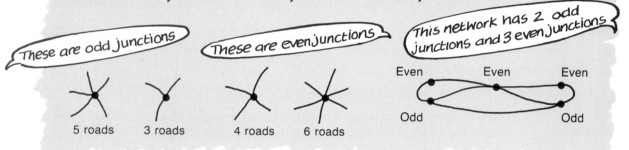

These are odd junctions

5 roads   3 roads

These are even junctions

4 roads   6 roads

This network has 2 odd
junctions and 3 even junctions

Even   Even   Even

Odd   Odd

2 Ismael thought about networks with only **even** junctions.
For each of the networks below:

(a) Check that **all** the junctions are even.
(b) Try to draw each network using the rules above.
(c) What do you notice about where you start and finish?
(d) Try to draw each network from a different starting point.
What do you notice about where you start and finish?

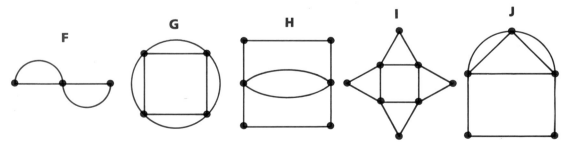

F   G   H   I   J

Using the rules, you can draw any network with all its junctions even.

3 Each network below has **some odd** junctions.

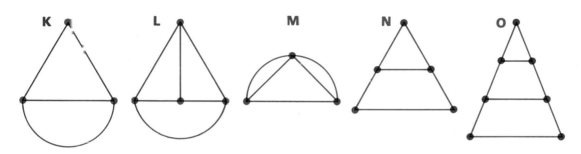

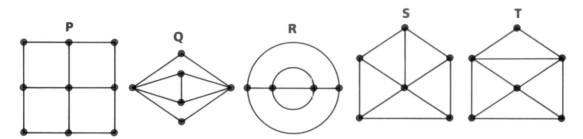

(a) Copy this table and complete it for each network in turn.

(b) How many odd junctions does each 'yes' network have?

(c) For these networks where do you start and finish?

Network	Number of odd junctions	Can it be drawn using the rules?
K	2	Yes

Using the rules, you can draw any network with *only two* odd junctions.

4 (a) Look at these junctions. Can you draw each network using the rules?
Check by drawing.

(b) If you can draw the network, at which junctions can you start and finish?

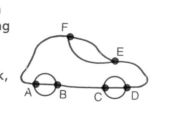

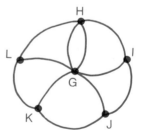

5 Ismael drew this map of his housing estate

(a) Investigate whether you could walk along all the roads **once only** starting and finishing in Maple Walk.

(b) Where would you have to start and finish, to walk along all the roads once only but leaving out Fir Circus?

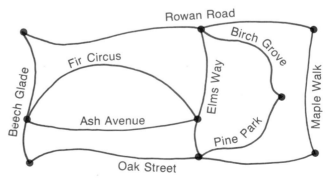

Ask your teacher what to do next.

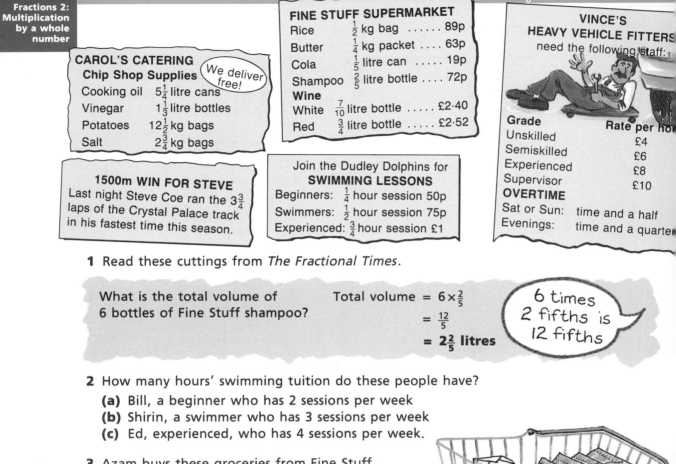

CAROL'S CATERING
Chip Shop Supplies *We deliver free!*
Cooking oil $5\frac{1}{4}$ litre cans
Vinegar $1\frac{1}{3}$ litre bottles
Potatoes $12\frac{1}{2}$ kg bags
Salt $2\frac{3}{4}$ kg bags

FINE STUFF SUPERMARKET
Rice $\frac{1}{2}$ kg bag 89p
Butter $\frac{1}{4}$ kg packet 63p
Cola $\frac{1}{5}$ litre can 19p
Shampoo $\frac{2}{5}$ litre bottle 72p
Wine
White $\frac{7}{10}$ litre bottle ..... £2·40
Red $\frac{3}{4}$ litre bottle ..... £2·52

VINCE'S HEAVY VEHICLE FITTERS
need the following staff:

Grade	Rate per hour
Unskilled	£4
Semiskilled	£6
Experienced	£8
Supervisor	£10

OVERTIME
Sat or Sun: time and a half
Evenings: time and a quarter

1500m WIN FOR STEVE
Last night Steve Coe ran the $3\frac{3}{4}$ laps of the Crystal Palace track in his fastest time this season.

Join the Dudley Dolphins for
SWIMMING LESSONS
Beginners: $\frac{1}{4}$ hour session 50p
Swimmers: $\frac{1}{2}$ hour session 75p
Experienced: $\frac{3}{4}$ hour session £1

1 Read these cuttings from *The Fractional Times*.

What is the total volume of 6 bottles of Fine Stuff shampoo?

Total volume $= 6 \times \frac{2}{5}$

$= \frac{12}{5}$

$= 2\frac{2}{5}$ **litres**

6 times 2 fifths is 12 fifths

2 How many hours' swimming tuition do these people have?
(a) Bill, a beginner who has 2 sessions per week
(b) Shirin, a swimmer who has 3 sessions per week
(c) Ed, experienced, who has 4 sessions per week.

3 Azam buys these groceries from Fine Stuff. Calculate the weight in kilograms of the
(a) rice   (b) butter   (c) rice **and** butter.

4 Anna goes to Fine Stuff for 6 cans of cola, 4 bottles of red wine and 5 bottles of white wine. Calculate the volume in litres of the
(a) cola   (b) red wine   (c) white wine   (d) red **and** white wine.

Carol's Catering Supplies delivered seven bags of salt to Fresh Fry Chip Shop. What was the total weight?

Total weight $= 7 \times 2\frac{3}{4}$

$= (7 \times 2) + (7 \times \frac{3}{4})$

$= 14 + \frac{21}{4}$

$= 14 + 5\frac{1}{4}$

$= 19\frac{1}{4}$ **kg**

7 lots of 2 is 14
7 lots of $\frac{3}{4}$ is 21 quarters

5 (a) What is the volume in litres of five cans of cooking oil?
(b) How many litres of vinegar are there in eight bottles?
(c) What is the total weight of potatoes in three bags?

6 Steve Coe ran twelve 1500 m races last season. How many laps of the track was that?

7 At Vince's how much would each grade of fitter earn for an hour of overtime
(a) on a Saturday or Sunday
(b) in the evening?

What does 'time and a half' mean?

Work for an hour and get paid for an hour and a half.

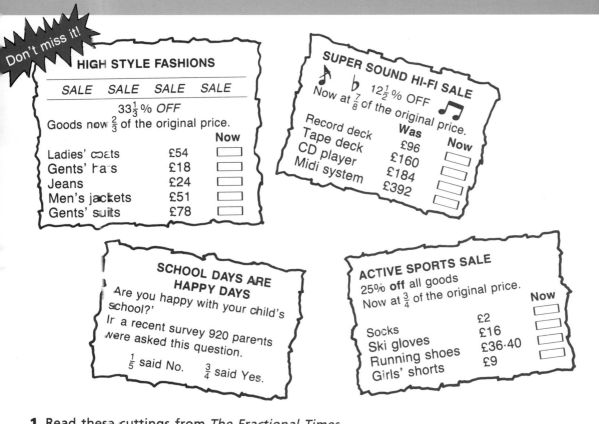

Don't miss it!

HIGH STYLE FASHIONS

SALE   SALE   SALE   SALE
$33\frac{1}{3}$% OFF
Goods now $\frac{2}{3}$ of the original price.

		Now
Ladies' coats	£54	☐
Gents' hats	£18	☐
Jeans	£24	☐
Men's jackets	£51	☐
Gents' suits	£78	☐

SUPER SOUND HI-FI SALE
$12\frac{1}{2}$% OFF
Now at $\frac{7}{8}$ of the original price.

	Was	**Now**
Record deck	£96	☐
Tape deck	£160	☐
CD player	£184	☐
Midi system	£392	☐

SCHOOL DAYS ARE HAPPY DAYS

'Are you happy with your child's school?'
In a recent survey 920 parents were asked this question.
$\frac{1}{5}$ said No. $\frac{3}{4}$ said Yes.

ACTIVE SPORTS SALE
25% **off** all goods
Now at $\frac{3}{4}$ of the original price.

		Now
Socks	£2	☐
Ski gloves	£16	☐
Running shoes	£36·40	☐
Girls' shorts	£9	☐

1 Read these cuttings from *The Fractional Times*.

What is the sale price of a lady's coat at High Style?

To find 1 third divide by 3 ⟶ $\frac{1}{3}$ of 54 = 18
To find 2 thirds multiply by 2 ⟶ $\frac{2}{3}$ of 54 = 18 × 2

   = **36**

The sale price of a lady's coat is **£36**.

2 Find the sale price of each of the other items at High Style.

3 What is the sale price of each item at Super Sound?

4 For each item in the sale at Active Sports find
   (a) the sale price
   (b) the amount you saved in the sale.

5 In the survey, how many parents **(a)** said no
                                       (b) said yes
                                       (c) did not reply?

6 Write out the ingredients for pineapple
ice cream to serve
   (a) 6 people **(b)** 8 people.

PARTY RECIPE ✱
Pineapple Icecream
Serves 12
1320 g fresh pineapple
180 g caster sugar
420 ml water
480 ml double cream
6 egg whites.

Jafar has 2 fifths of 1 bar of chocolate.
Jane has 1 fifth of 2 bars.
They both have the same amount.

So $\frac{2}{5} = \frac{1}{5}$ of $2 = 2 \div 5 = 0.4$

$$\begin{array}{r} 0.4 \\ 5\overline{\smash{)}2.0} \end{array}$$

Fatima has 3 quarters of 1 bar of toffee.
Fred has 1 quarter of 3 bars.
They both have the same amount.

So $\frac{3}{4} = \frac{1}{4}$ of $3 = 3 \div 4 = 0.75$

$$\begin{array}{r} 0.75 \\ 4\overline{\smash{)}3.00} \end{array}$$

To find the decimal form of a fraction, divide the numerator by the denominator.

1 Find the decimal form of each of these fractions **by dividing**.
    (a) $\frac{1}{2}$ **(b)** $\frac{3}{5}$ **(c)** $\frac{1}{4}$ **(d)** $\frac{1}{5}$ **(e)** $\frac{4}{5}$

Use a calculator.

To find the decimal form of $\frac{3}{8}$ Press **3** **÷** **8** **=** to give **0.375**

2 Find the decimal form of
    (a) $\frac{1}{8}$ **(b)** $\frac{5}{8}$ **(c)** $\frac{7}{8}$ **(d)** $\frac{9}{25}$ **(e)** $\frac{19}{40}$ **(f)** $\frac{11}{16}$

3 (a) What answer does the calculator show for
      the decimal form of $\frac{1}{3}$?
  (b) What do you **think** the calculator will show for $\frac{2}{3}$?
      Check using your calculator.

4 What answer does the calculator show for
    (a) $\frac{1}{9}$ **(b)** $\frac{2}{9}$ **(c)** $\frac{3}{9}$?

5 What do you **think** the calculator will show for
    (a) $\frac{4}{9}$ **(b)** $\frac{5}{9}$ **(c)** $\frac{6}{9}$ **(d)** $\frac{7}{9}$ **(e)** $\frac{8}{9}$?
  Check using your calculator.

6 What answer does the calculator show for
    (a) $\frac{1}{11}$ **(b)** $\frac{2}{11}$ **(c)** $\frac{3}{11}$ **(d)** $\frac{4}{11}$ **(e)** $\frac{5}{11}$?

7 What do you **think** the calculator will show for
    (a) $\frac{6}{11}$ **(b)** $\frac{7}{11}$ **(c)** $\frac{8}{11}$ **(d)** $\frac{9}{11}$ **(e)** $\frac{10}{11}$?
  Check using your calculator.

8 Investigate the decimal form of $\frac{1}{99}, \frac{2}{99}, \frac{3}{99}, \ldots$

Ask your teacher what to do next.

Shorthand!

You can use a dot above a digit to
show that it repeats:

$16 \div 9 = 1.7777777 \rightarrow 1.\dot{7}$

When more than one digit repeats
use two dots:

$116 \div 99 = 1.1717171 \rightarrow 1.\dot{1}\dot{7}$

$123 \div 999 = 0.1231231 \rightarrow 0.\dot{1}2\dot{3}$

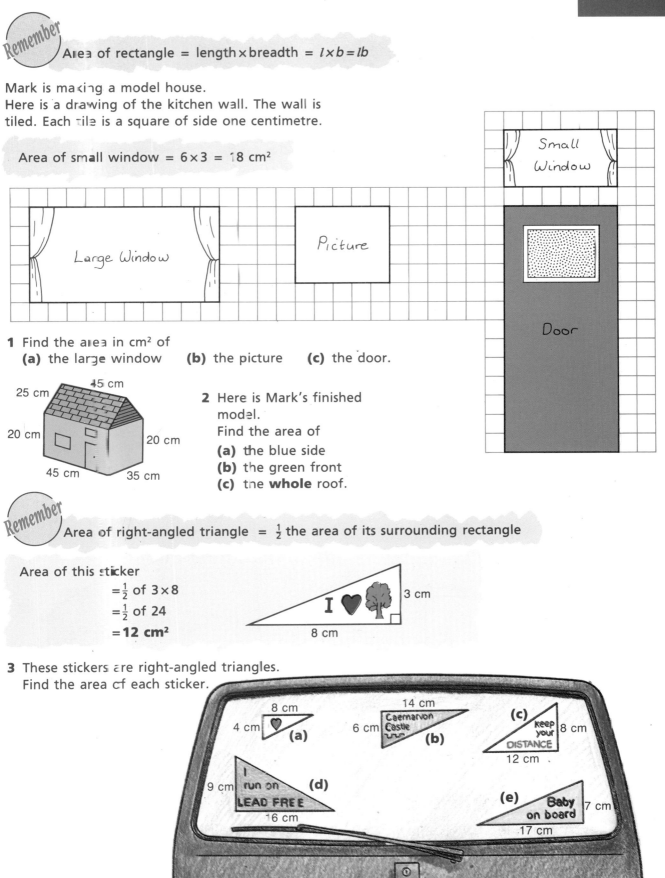

Remember

Area of rectangle = length × breadth = $l \times b = lb$

Mark is making a model house.
Here is a drawing of the kitchen wall. The wall is tiled. Each tile is a square of side one centimetre.

Area of small window = 6 × 3 = 18 cm²

1 Find the area in cm² of
   (a) the large window   **(b)** the picture   **(c)** the door.

2 Here is Mark's finished model.
   Find the area of
   (a) the blue side
   (b) the green front
   (c) the **whole** roof.

Remember

Area of right-angled triangle = $\frac{1}{2}$ the area of its surrounding rectangle

Area of this sticker
$$= \frac{1}{2} \text{ of } 3 \times 8$$
$$= \frac{1}{2} \text{ of } 24$$
$$= \textbf{12 cm}^2$$

3 These stickers are right-angled triangles.
   Find the area of each sticker.

Ayoko is making a stained glass panel using pieces of coloured glass. She sells them to people to hang in their windows.

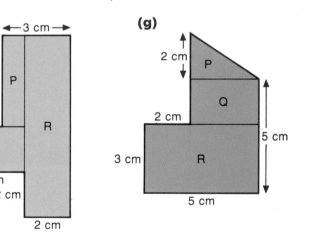

1 This green area of glass is made from a rectangle and a triangle.

Copy and complete:

Area of rectangle P = ☐ × ☐ = ☐ cm²

Area of triangle Q = $\frac{1}{2}$ × ☐ × ☐ = ☐ cm²

Area of green glass = ☐ cm²

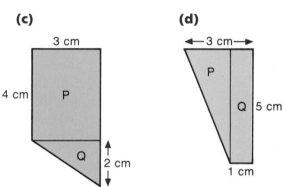

2 In the same way find the area of each of these glass shapes.

(a)

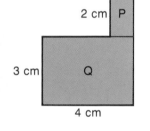
1 cm
2 cm P
3 cm
Q
4 cm

(b)
5 cm
P
4 cm
Q
2 cm
3 cm

(c)
3 cm
4 cm P
Q
2 cm

(d)
← 3 cm →
P
Q 5 cm
1 cm

(e)
← 9 cm →
2 cm
P
Q 4 cm
4 cm R
2 cm
2 cm

(f)
← 3 cm →
4 cm P
R
2 cm Q
3 cm
2 cm
2 cm

(g)
2 cm P
Q
2 cm
3 cm R
5 cm
5 cm

3 What is the total area of Ayoko's stained glass?

4 Find the length and breadth of Ayoko's stained glass panel. Explain how you can use these to check your answer to question **3**.

Motif Unlimited supplies decorative
patches for clothing. Ian calculates how
much material he needs for each motif.

1 For this jean's patch calculate the area of

   (a) the red triangle
   (b) the blue triangle
   (c) the **large** triangle made from the
        red **and** blue triangles.

2 Check that the area of this large triangle
   is **half** the area of the rectangular patch.

2cm

←2cm→←   3cm   →

Area of triangle = $\frac{1}{2}$ the area of its surrounding rectangle

   = $\frac{1}{2}$ of length × breadth

   = $\frac{1}{2}$ of base × height

   = $\frac{1}{2}$ × b × h

Area of triangle = $\frac{1}{2} bh$

height, h

← base, b →

In a triangle the base and height are **perpendicular** to each other

h
b

b
h

h
b

b
h

3 Calculate the area of each
   triangular patch like this:

4 cm

← 5 cm →

Area = $\frac{1}{2} bh$

   = $\frac{1}{2}$ × 5 × 4

   = 10 cm²

The patch has an area of **10 cm²**

(a)

7 cm

←4 cm→

(b)

+3 cm+

←6 cm→

(c)

8 cm

← 5 cm →

(d)

5.5 cm

← 6 cm →

←   8.5 cm   →

(e)

9 cm

2 cm

(f)

7 cm

3 cm

(g)

5 cm

5 cm

(h)

10 cm

4 Do Workbook page 33.

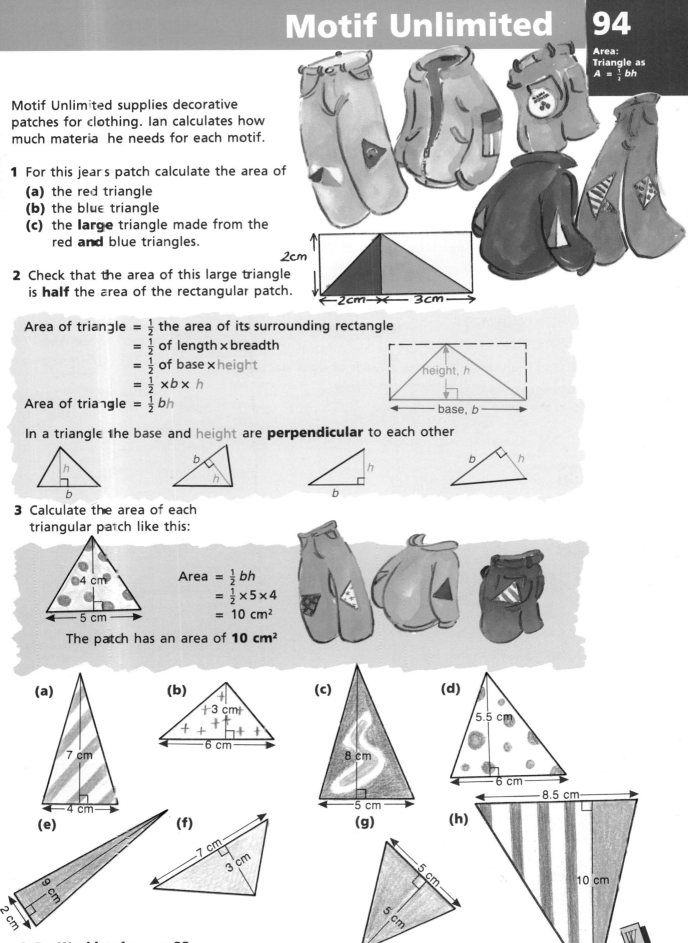

Maggie Carter helps customers work out prices and how much to buy.

What area will one litre of Wonderpaint cover?

Paint in litres	Area in m²
5	65
1	65 ÷ 5 = **13**

One litre will cover **13 m²**.

1 What area will one litre of each of these paints cover?

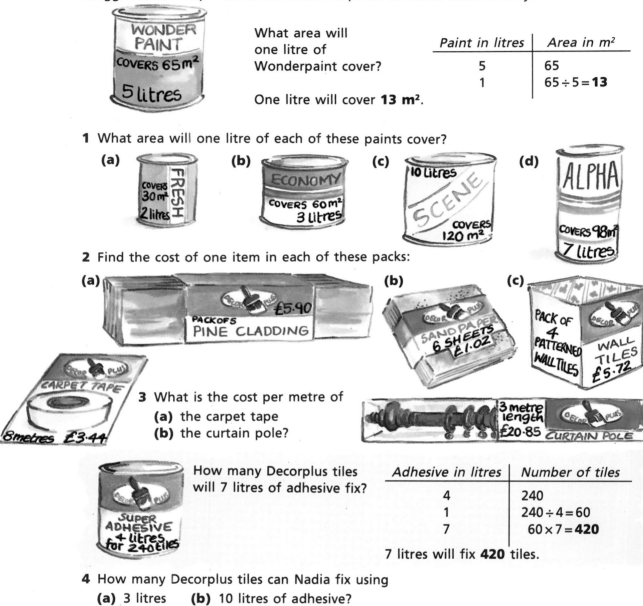

(a) FRESH COVERS 30 m² 2 litres

(b) ECONOMY COVERS 60 m² 3 litres

(c) 10 litres SCENE COVERS 120 m²

(d) ALPHA COVERS 98 m² 7 litres

2 Find the cost of one item in each of these packs:

(a) PACK OF 5 PINE CLADDING £5.90

(b) SAND PAPER 6 SHEETS £1.02

(c) PACK OF 4 PATTERNED WALL TILES £5.72

CARPET TAPE 8 metres £3.44

3 What is the cost per metre of
(a) the carpet tape
(b) the curtain pole?

3 metre length £20.85 CURTAIN POLE

How many Decorplus tiles will 7 litres of adhesive fix?

SUPER ADHESIVE 4 litres for 240 tiles

Adhesive in litres	Number of tiles
4	240
1	240 ÷ 4 = 60
7	60 × 7 = **420**

7 litres will fix **420** tiles.

4 How many Decorplus tiles can Nadia fix using
(a) 3 litres   (b) 10 litres of adhesive?

5 Find the cost of eight items in each of the following:

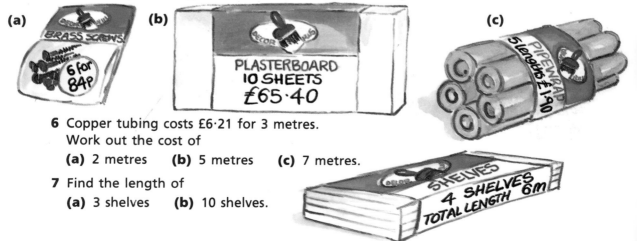

(a) BRASS SCREWS 6 for 84p

(b) PLASTERBOARD 10 SHEETS £65.40

(c) PIPEWRAP 5 lengths £1.90

6 Copper tubing costs £6.21 for 3 metres.
Work out the cost of
(a) 2 metres   (b) 5 metres   (c) 7 metres.

7 Find the length of
(a) 3 shelves   (b) 10 shelves.

SHELVES 4 SHELVES TOTAL LENGTH 6m

Twenty sheets of Decorplus plywood costs £84. How much does one sheet cost?

Number of sheets	Cost in £
20	84
1	$84 \div 20 = \mathbf{4 \cdot 2}$

$84 \div 2 \rightarrow 42$
$42 \div 10 \rightarrow 4 \cdot 2$

So 1 sheet costs **£4·20**

1 Find the cost of **one** item in each of these:

(a)

PAVING SLABS
40 for
£98·40

(b)

FACING
BRICKS
50 for £21

(c)

WALL PLUGS
WALL PLUGS
80 for £1·60

(d)

300 for
£4·20   STEEL SCREWS

30 nails weigh 510 grams. What do 48 nails weigh?

Number of nails	Weight in g
30	510
1	$510 \div 30 = 17$
48	$17 \times 48 = \mathbf{816}$

$$\begin{array}{r} 17 \\ \times 48 \\ \hline 136 \\ 680 \\ \hline 816 \end{array}$$

48 nails weigh 816 grams

2 What is the weight of   **(a)** 25 nails   **(b)** 72 nails?

3 Tony wants 18 tiles. Find the cost in each case.

(a)

BETTATILE
£22·40
20 TILES

(b)

AROTILE
£63·00 60 TILES

(c)

K-TILE
£41·50   50 TILES

If 50 Decorplus tacks cost 35p, how much do 20 cost?

Number of Tacks	Costing Price
50	35
10	$35 \div 5 = 7$
20	$7 \times 2 = 14$

Well 10 cost 7p so 20 cost 14p

4 For each length of screw find the cost of **30**.

(a)

40 for 48p
20 mm

(b)

100 for £1·70
25 mm

(c)

80 for £5·12
40 mm

5 A packet of two hinges costs £1·75. How much do ten hinges cost?

6 Twelve sheets of chipboard cover 17 m² of floor.
What floor area will these cover? **(a)** 6 sheets   **(b)** 48 sheets   **(c)** 120 sheets.

Best buy at Decorplus

1 Decorplus white spirit comes in four sizes.
  (a) For each size work out the cost of one litre.
  (b) Which size seems to be the best value?
  (c) What is the cheapest way to buy 4 litres
     of white spirit? Explain your answer.

2 (a) Which size of paint
    is the better value?
    Explain your answer.
  (b) Why do you think
    Azad bought the
    2 litre tin?

3 Decorplus sells packets of all-purpose
filler singly or by the box.
  (a) Which is the better value?
  (b) What is the cheapest way of buying
    10 packets of filler? How much do they cost?

4 Lengths of ceiling coving cost £2·90 each
or £14·40 for a pack of six.
  (a) Which is the better value?
  (b) Work out the cheapest way to buy • 7 lengths
    • 11 lengths.
    Explain your answers.

5 (a) Which bag of cement is the better
    value?
  (b) Pete needs 28 kg of cement.
    Which bags should he buy?
    Explain your answer.

6 Decorplus has four brands of top-quality carpet tiles.

  (a) Which brand of carpet seems to be the best buy?
    Explain your answer.
  (b) Decorplus only sells the tiles in complete boxes.
    Mrs Sanderson needs 34 tiles. Calculate how much each
    brand would cost her.
  (c) Which brand should she choose? Is this the same as your
    answer to part (a)? Explain.

Ask your teacher what to do next.

How do you think factories make different shaped boxes?
They start with a **net**.

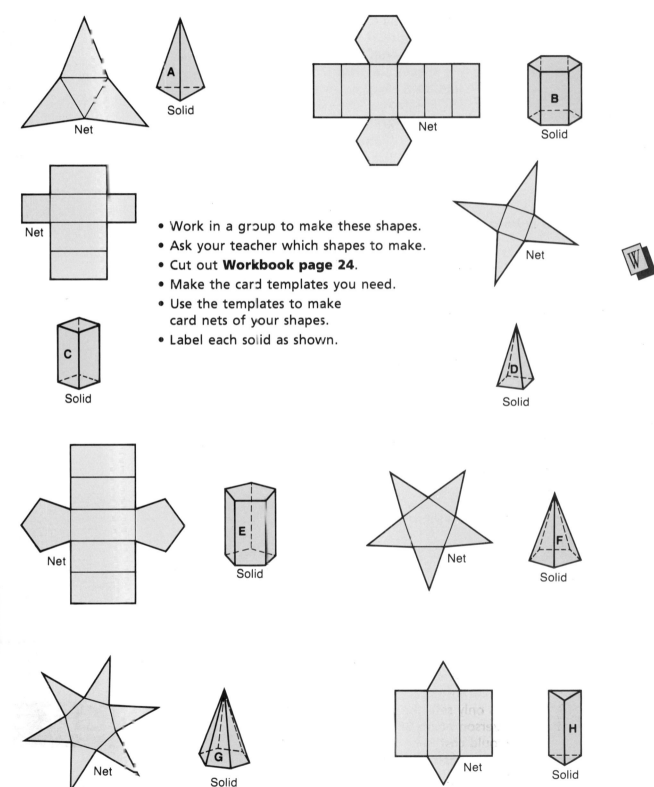

- Work in a group to make these shapes.
- Ask your teacher which shapes to make.
- Cut out **Workbook page 24**.
- Make the card templates you need.
- Use the templates to make
  card nets of your shapes.
- Label each solid as shown.

Keep your shapes for Textbook pages 99 and 100.

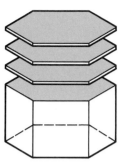

You need the shapes your group made from Textbook page 98.

1 Shape **B** is a **prism**. You can slice it like this.
The orange faces are **identical hexagons**.
Shape **B** is called a **hexagonal prism**.
Which of the other shapes are prisms?
Name each one like this: Shape **B** – hexagonal prism

2 Shape **G** is a **pyramid**. The blue faces are hexagons of **the same shape but different sizes**. Shape **G** is called a **hexagonal pyramid**. Which of the other shapes are pyramids? Name each one.

3 This **cuboid** can also be called a **rectangular prism**.

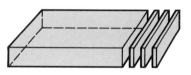

Give a different name for each of the following shapes.

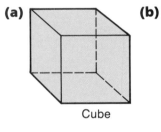
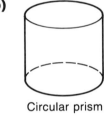
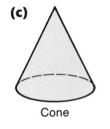
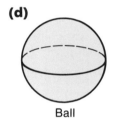

(a)	**(b)**	**(c)**	**(d)**
Cube	Circular prism	Cone	Ball

4 Name all the shapes used to make each of these lamps.
Some shapes are not complete.

(a)   **(b)**   **(c)**

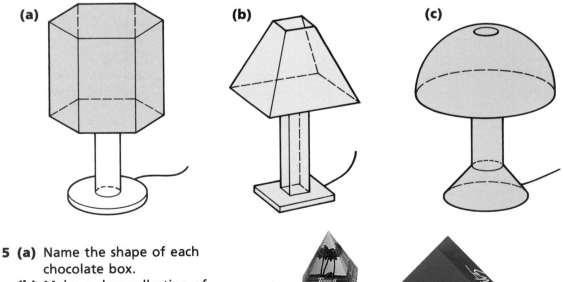

5 (a) Name the shape of each chocolate box.
(b) Make a class collection of containers with interesting shapes.

Keep the shapes your group made for Textbook page 100.

Looking at shapes

100

3D shape:
Faces,
vertices,
edges

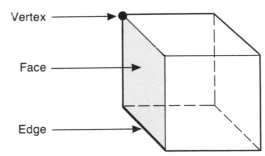

Vertex

Face

Edge

A cube has 8 vertices (corners)
6 faces (surfaces)
12 edges.

You need the shapes your group made from Textbook page 98.

1 (a) Copy and complete a
table like this for all your
shapes.
(b) What do you notice
about the numbers in the
last two columns of your
table? Try to write this as
a formula.
(c) Ask your teacher about the
Swiss mathematician,
Leonhard Euler.

	Shape	Number of			faces + vertices
		faces	vertices	edges	
	Cube	6	8	12	14
A	Triangular pyramid				
B	Hexagonal prism				
C					
D					

2 Which of the shapes below are **(a)** pyramids **(b)** prisms?

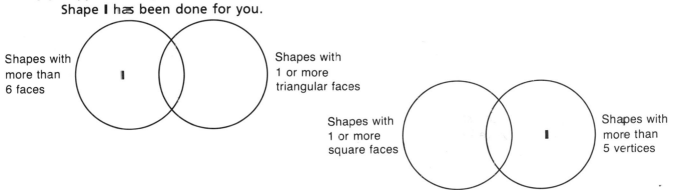

I   J   K   L   M   N   O

3 Shape I has 3 faces, 12 vertices and 18 edges. Which of the shapes have
(a) more than 6 faces **(b)** more than 5 vertices **(c)** less than 12 edges
(d) exactly 6 vertices **(e)** 1 or more triangular faces **(f)** 1 or more square faces?

4 (a) Copy and complete these diagrams by entering the letter of each shape.
Shape I has been done for you.

Shapes with
more than
6 faces

I

Shapes with
1 or more
triangular faces

Shapes with
1 or more
square faces

I

Shapes with
more than
5 vertices

(b) Describe the shapes in the part of each diagram where the circles overlap.

Cut out Workbook pages 26 and 27.
Ask your teacher which puzzle your group should make.

Red puzzle

- Use a pin to prick through **net A** on to card.

- Cut **two** pieces of card to match **net A**.

- Fold each net along the dotted lines.

- Join the edges to make **two** shapes.

- Place the **two** shapes together to make a **triangular pyramid**.

Blue puzzle

- Use a pin to prick through **net B** on to card.

- Cut **three** pieces of card to match **net B**.

- Fold each net along the dotted lines.

- Join the edges to make **three** shapes.

- Place the **three** shapes together to make a **cube**.

Yellow puzzle

- Use a pin to prick through **net C** on to card.

- Cut **six** pieces of card to match **net C**.

- Fold each net along the dotted lines.

- Join the edges to make **six square pyramids**.

- Place the **six** shapes together to make a **cube**.

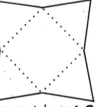

Green puzzle

- Use a pin to prick through **net D** on to card.

- Cut **four** pieces of card to match **net D**.

- Fold each net along the dotted lines.

- Join the edges to make **four triangular pyramids**.

- Place the **four** shapes together to make a **square pyramid**.

- Use the large dotted triangle on **net D** to make a net like this.

- Fold your net and join the edges to make a **triangular pyramid**.

- Place all **five** shapes together to make a **cube**.

Ask your teacher what to do next.

Channel Prince is a
passenger ferry. Here is the
booking office passenger record
for last week.

Sun	473
Mon	1849
Tues	1587
Wed	1282
Thur	1017
Fri	1851
Sat	825

How many passengers altogether did Channel Prince carry on Sunday and Monday?

You can find an **approximate** answer **mentally** by rounding **to the nearest 100**.
473 + 1849 is about 500 + 1800, that is **about 2300**.

You can find an **exact** answer by calculator. 473 + 1849 is **exactly 2322**.

The approximate answer, about 2300, shows that
the calculator answer is likely to be correct.

1 Find the approximate answers mentally, and the exact answers by calculator.
How many passengers altogether did Channel Prince carry on
(a) Saturday and Sunday   (b) Wednesday and Thursday
(c) Friday Saturday and Sunday?

2 The captain of Channel Prince keeps this record.

	Week 1	Week 2	Week 3	Week 4	Week 5	Week 6	Week 7	Week 8
Number of passengers carried	6096	3498	5866	2505	957	8262	4752	2023
Number of crossings	16	11	14	5	3	18	9	7

Find approximate answers mentally by rounding
to the nearest 1000 and exact answers by calculator.
How many **more** passengers did Channel Prince carry in
(a) week 1 than in week 2   (b) week 3 than in week 4
(c) week 6 than in week 7 and week 8 together?

3 The captain calculates that the average number of passengers
carried per crossing in week 1 was 6096 ÷ 16, that is 381.
He checks his calculator answers **by multiplying** without clearing the display.

Enter `6096`   `÷ 1 6 =` → `381.`   Check `× 1 6 =` → `6096.`

Find the average number the ship carried per crossing in
(a) week 2   (b) week 4   (c) week 6.
Check your answers by multiplying.

4 (a) Press `1 ÷ 6 × 6 =`   The answer might surprise you!

1 ÷ 6 is equal to 0·166 666 666 666 6... and so on.

Some calculators • display 1 ÷ 6 as 0·166 666 6
              • **ignore** all the other sixes
              • find 0·166 666 6 × 6 which is
                0·999 999 6

(b) Investigate these:
• 5 ÷ 6 × 6
• 1 ÷ 3 × 3
• 32 ÷ 9 × 9

Ask your teacher what to do next.

Patti's Punch
2 litres
   lemonade
1 litre
   orange juice
300 ml
   lemon juice

1 litre = 1000 millilitres (1000 ml)

Patti is having a christening party for her baby, Joe. She makes some punch.

1 What is the total volume of Patti's punch in
  (a) litres   **(b)** millilitres?

2 A glass holds 100 ml. How many glasses can Patti fill from a bowl of punch?

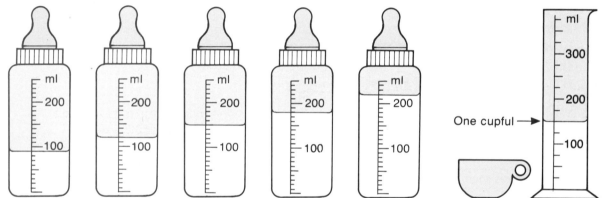

0 to 2 weeks   2 to 8 weeks   2 to 3 months   3 to 6 months   6 to 12 months

One cupful →

3 These bottles show the volumes of feed for babies of different ages.
  (a) Write the volume of feed in each bottle.
  (b) Which of these feeds are more than one cupful?
  (c) Joe is 4 months old and has 5 feeds a day. How many cupfuls is this?
  (d) Jackie next door is 8 months old and has 3 feeds per day.
     Write, in litres, the total volume of feed Jackie has in one week.

1 millilitre (1 ml) = 1 cubic centimetre (1 cm³)

4 A 500 ml measuring jar contains oil. Gary puts a metal ball into the oil.
  (a) What was the oil level before and after Gary put in the ball?
  (b) What is the volume in cm³ of the ball?
  (c) How many **more** balls can he add **before** the oil overflows?

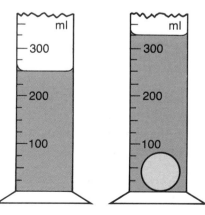

Remember

For every cuboid
$V = l \times b \times h$

Cuboid	l in cm	b in cm	h in cm
A	4	4	3
B	5	4	2
C	6	5	4
D	10	10	10

1 (a) Find the volume of the cuboids
   A, **B**, **C** and **D**.
(b) Give another name for cuboid **D**.

2 Write the volumes of the **cubes** with these edge lengths:

   (a) 1 cm   **(b)** 2 cm   **(c)** 3 cm   **(d)** 4 cm   **(e)** 5 cm   **(f)** 6 cm

3 Joyce Lo finds a small cardboard box
   6 cm long, 4 cm broad and 3 cm deep.
   (a) How many centimetre cubes could
   she pack into the box?
   (b) How many millilitres of sand could
   she put in the box?

Work in a small group for questions 4 and 5.

4 (a) Ask your teacher for a toothpaste
   box. Measure, to the nearest
   centimetre, its length, breadth and
   height. Find the approximate
   volume of the box.
(b) Write the volume of the box in
   millilitres.
(c) Find the difference between this
   volume and the volume marked in
   ml on the toothpaste box.

5 (a) Make an open cardboard box from
   a net like this. What volume of
   sand would it contain if you filled
   it level to the top?

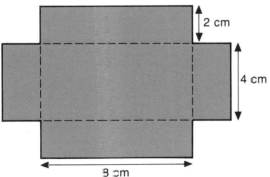

2 cm

4 cm

8 cm

(b) Make another cardboard box with
   different length, breadth and
   height, to hold the **same volume**
   of sand.
(c) What is the edge length of a **cube**
   with this same volume?

You need three metre sticks, drawing pins and string.

Work as a group in a corner.

1 (a) Make a cube as shown with edge length 1 metre.

The cube you have made has a volume of 1 cubic metre.

(b) Find out if all your group can fit inside the metre cube at the same time.

A cube with edge length 1 metre has a volume of 1 cubic metre or 1 m³. Other shapes can have a volume of 1 m³.

1 m³ concrete

2 (a) Estimate the volume, in cubic metres, of your classroom.
(b) Measure, to the nearest metre, the length, breadth and height of your classroom.
(c) Calculate the approximate volume, in cubic metres, of your classroom.
(d) Find the difference, in cubic metres, between your estimated and calculated volumes.

3 Find the volume, in cubic metres, of each of these.

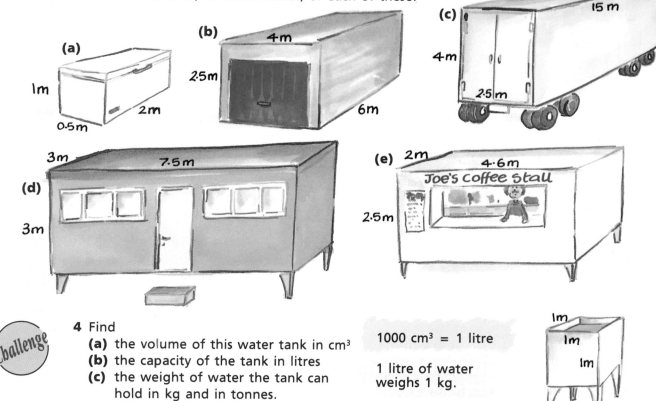

(a) 1 m, 2 m, 0·5 m

(b) 4 m, 2·5 m, 6 m

(c) 15 m, 4 m, 2·5 m

(d) 3 m, 7·5 m, 3 m

(e) 2 m, 4·6 m, 2·5 m   Joe's coffee stall

Challenge

4 Find
  (a) the volume of this water tank in cm³
  (b) the capacity of the tank in litres
  (c) the weight of water the tank can hold in kg and in tonnes.

1000 cm³ = 1 litre

1 litre of water weighs 1 kg.

1 m, 1 m, 1 m

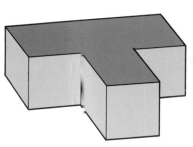

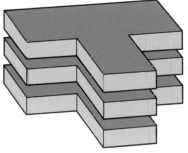

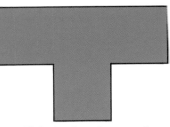

This solid can be cut into identical slices. It is called a **prism**.

The red faces show the **cross-section**.

This is the shape of the **cross-section**.

1 Think about cutting these prisms into identical slices.
Draw the shape of the cross-sections.

(a)   **(b)**   **(c)**   **(d)**   **(e)**

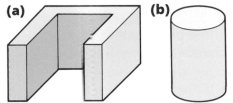

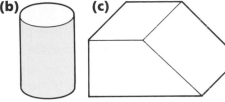

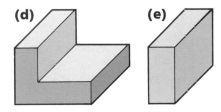

2 Julie gives her younger brother this toy. The prisms fit the holes in the yellow plate. He pushes them into the Plasticine to make the shapes of the cross-sections.

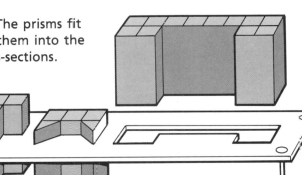

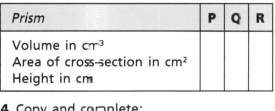

Plasticine

(a) On squared paper draw the shape each prism makes on the Plasticine.
(b) Write the area, in square units, of each cross-section.

3 These prisms are made from centimetre cubes.
   (a) Count the cubes to find the volume of each prism.
   (b) Copy and complete the table.

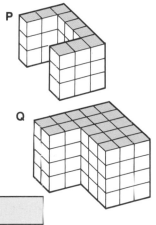

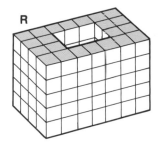

P

Q

R

Prism	P	Q	R
Volume in cm³			
Area of cross-section in cm²			
Height in cm			

4 Copy and complete:

Volume of prism =   &boxempty;   ×   &boxempty;

Ask your teacher what to do next.

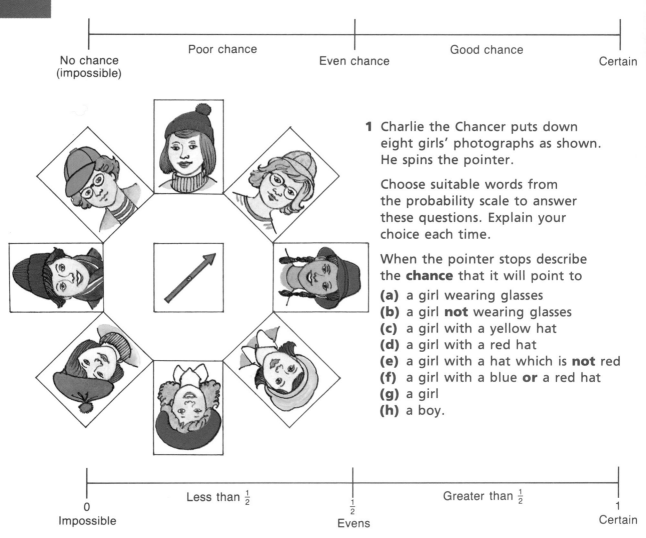

Poor chance — Good chance

No chance (impossible) — Even chance — Certain

1 Charlie the Chancer puts down eight girls' photographs as shown. He spins the pointer.

Choose suitable words from the probability scale to answer these questions. Explain your choice each time.

When the pointer stops describe the **chance** that it will point to

(a) a girl wearing glasses

(b) a girl **not** wearing glasses

(c) a girl with a yellow hat

(d) a girl with a red hat

(e) a girl with a hat which is **not** red

(f) a girl with a blue **or** a red hat

(g) a girl

(h) a boy.

0 — Less than ½ — ½ — Greater than ½ — 1

Impossible — Evens — Certain

2 Charlie puts these boys' photographs **face down**.

Choose words **and** numbers from the probability scale to answer these questions. Explain your choice each time.

When Charlie turns over a photograph **at random**, what is the probability that it will be

(a) a boy aged 12

(b) a boy not aged 12

(c) a boy with initial A

(d) a boy whose initial is not A

(e) a boy with initial J

(f) a boy whose initial is not J

(g) a boy aged 11 with initial A

(h) a boy

(i) a girl?

John — Age 12

Asif — Age 11

Nick — Age 12

Ahmed — Age 13

Jim — Age 12

Joe — Age 12

This bag contains 1 green, 2 blue and 9 red beads.
Anne picks a bead from the bag.

There is a poor chance that she will pick green.

The probability of picking a green bead from the bag is 1 in 12 or $\frac{1}{12}$

There is a good chance that she will pick red.

The probability of picking a red bead from the bag is 9 in 12 or $\frac{9}{12} = \frac{3}{4}$

1 What is the probability that Anne will pick a blue bead?

2 This bag contains 10 beads. What is the probability of picking a bead which is
   (a) blue   **(b)** green   **(c)** red   **(d)** yellow?

3 If you roll a die, what is the probability that you will get
   (a) a six   **(b)** a four   **(c)** an odd number?

4 If you shuffle these cards and place them face down on a table, what is the probability that you will pick
   (a) an A   **(b)** an E   **(c)** an M?

E M M A

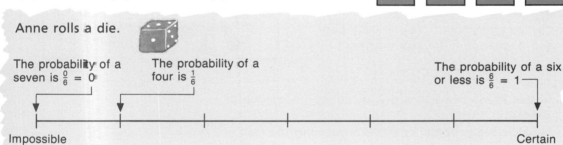

Anne rolls a die.

The probability of a seven is $\frac{0}{6} = 0$

The probability of a four is $\frac{1}{6}$

The probability of a six or less is $\frac{6}{6} = 1$

Impossible   Certain

5 (a) Copy this **probability scale**.

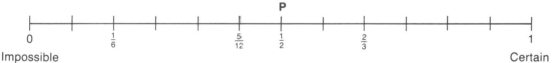

P

0    $\frac{1}{6}$ $\frac{5}{12}$ $\frac{1}{2}$ $\frac{2}{3}$ 1

Impossible   Certain

   (b) Find the probability for each of these situations.
   Match the letter with one probability on your scale. **P** has been done for you.
   P When a coin is tossed what's the probability of a head?
   Q When a die is rolled what is the probability of a six?
   R When a die is rolled what is the probability of scoring less than 5?
   S Four cards are lettered A, E, I and U. What is the probability of picking a vowel?
   T A bag has 5 blue pegs, 3 green pegs and 4 red pegs. What is the probability of picking a blue peg?
   U A bag has 5 white pegs. What is the probability of picking a brown peg?

   (c) List **P** to **U** in order from most likely to least likely.

1 Jimmy spins the **Super-Spinner**. When it stops, what is the probability that the arrow will point to

    (a) red   **(b)** green   **(c)** blue   **(d)** white?

2 Jameela spins the **Card Carousel**. When it stops, what is the probability of the arrow pointing to a

    (a) five   **(b)** Queen   **(c)** diamond
    (d) three   **(e)** red card   **(f)** ten?

3 Twelve envelopes are pinned to this board.
- 3 contain a red card
- 2 contain a green card
- 6 contain a blue card
- 1 contains a white card

If you hit one of the envelopes, what is the probability that the card inside is

    (a) white   **(b)** blue   **(c)** red or blue
    (d) green   **(e)** not green   **(f)** yellow?

4 Marshall spins the **Wheel of Fortune**. What is the probability that he will win

    (a) a cuddly toy   **(b)** a lucky bag
    (c) a balloon   **(d)** nothing?

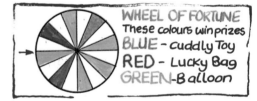

WHEEL OF FORTUNE
These colours win prizes
BLUE – Cuddly Toy
RED – Lucky Bag
GREEN – Balloon

5 In this **Hunt-the-Pea** a pea is hidden under one of the pots.
What is the probability of Pete guessing the pot

    (a) correctly   **(b)** incorrectly?

HUNT-THE-PEA

6 Tina runs the **Tombola stall**. At the end of the fair she has sold raffle tickets from these three books.

30 tickets Sold   25 tickets Sold

    (a) How many red tickets has she sold?
    (b) How many tickets has she sold altogether?
    (c) Omar bought one ticket. What is the probability that he will win first prize?

7 What is the probability that the winning Tombola ticket is

    (a) blue   **(b)** green   **(c)** red
    (d) yellow   **(e)** red or blue   **(f)** not blue?

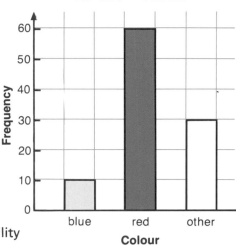

100 cars – colours

Class 2 tried to find out if Janice was right. They used data collection sheets to record the colour of the first 100 cars to pass the school gates. They drew this graph to show their results.

1 (a) How many of the cars were red?
   (b) What fraction of the cars were red?
   (c) Based on this data, estimate the probability that a car passing the gates will be red.
   (d) Is there a poor chance, an even chance, or a good chance that it will be red?

2 Repeat question **1** for the blue cars.

3 (a) Estimate the probability that a car passing the gates will be neither red nor blue.
   (b) Is there a poor chance, an even chance, or a good chance that it will be neither red nor blue?

4 (a) If Class 2 did this investigation again do you think their results would be the same? Explain.
   (b) Was Janice right about the most common car colour? Explain.

	Total
Cars	﷼﷼ ﷼﷼ ﷼﷼ ﷼﷼ ﷼﷼ ﷼﷼ ﷼﷼ ﷼﷼ ﷼﷼ ﷼﷼
Buses	﷼﷼ ﷼﷼
Lorries	﷼﷼ ﷼﷼ ﷼﷼ ﷼﷼
Others	﷼﷼ ﷼﷼ ﷼﷼ ﷼﷼

5 Class 2 collected information about the first **100 vehicles** to pass the school gates.
Here is part of Ajit's data sheet.

Of these 100 vehicles how many were
(a) cars   **(b)** buses
(c) lorries   **(d)** others?

6 Based on this data, estimate the probability that a vehicle passing the school gates will be
(a) a car   **(b)** a bus   **(c)** a lorry   **(d)** something else.

7 Collect your own data. Estimate the probability that a car passing **your** school gates will be red.

Challenge

When a die or spinner is **fair** each number has an **equal chance** of showing.

When a die or spinner has **bias** some numbers are **more likely** to show than others.

Experiment 1

You need scissors, glue and cm squared paper.

(a) Copy this net, cut it out and make the die.

(b) When the die is rolled, which numbers do you **think** are
• more likely • less likely?

(c) Roll the die 60 times. Record your results in a frequency table.

(d) Draw a bar chart of your results.

(e) Do you think this is a fair die? Explain.

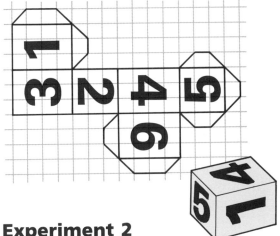

Experiment 2

You need scissors, glue, card, isometric dot paper and a matchstick.

(a) Copy the hexagon, glue it on to card and cut it out. Push the matchstick through the centre to make a spinner.

(b) When the spinner is spun do you **think** one number is more likely than any other? Explain.

(c) Spin the spinner 60 times. Record your results in a frequency table.

(d) Draw a bar chart of your results.

(e) Do you think this is a fair spinner? Discuss this with your teacher.

Experiment 3

You need scissors, glue, isometric dot paper and a drawing pin.

(a) Copy this net, cut it out and make the die.

(b) Stick a drawing pin in the middle of the face with the 3.

(c) When the die is rolled, which number do you **think** is most likely to be face down?

(d) Roll the die 60 times. Record your results in a frequency table.

(e) Draw a bar chart of your results.

(f) Do you think this is a fair die? Explain.

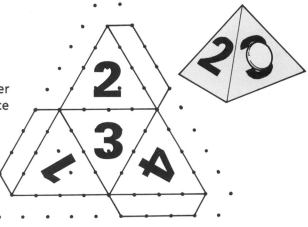

1 Supersleuth uses many items of disguise.
He has

2 pairs of glasses: dark (D), clear (C)
and 3 jackets: red (r), green (g), blue (b)

List the **six** different ways he can make up his disguise.

This **tree diagram** shows the six ways
that Supersleuth can make up his disguise.

The green branch shows Dr (dark glasses, red jacket).
The **thick** branch shows Cg (clear glasses, green jacket).

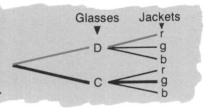

2 Copy and complete these tree diagrams and lists to show
different ways that Supersleuth can disguise himself.

(a) 3 umbrellas: grey (G), black (B),
red (R)
2 pipes: straight (s), curved (c)

(b) 2 hats: beret (B), deerstalker (D)
2 moustaches: handlebar (h), pencil (p)
3 face marks: mole (M), scar (S), wart (W)

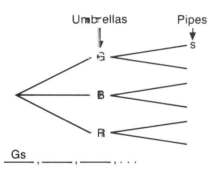

Gs ____, ____, ____, . . .

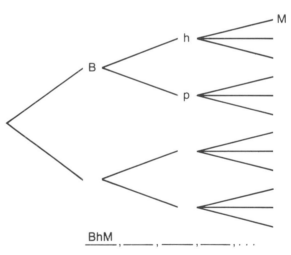

BhM ____, ____, ____, ____, . . .

3 Supersleuth uses two spinners to decide
which items to wear. These spinners
show that he should put on a long wig.

Draw a tree diagram and then list all
the possible outcomes from the two
spinners.

4 • Make two spinners like Supersleuth's
but choose your own items of
disguise.
• Draw a tree diagram to show all the
possible combined outcomes for your
spinners.
• How many times do you **think** you
would have to spin the spinners so
that each possible outcome occurred
at least once?
Choose from: A—less than 12,
B—exactly 12, C—more than 12.
• Find out!

Ask your teacher what to do next.

Down at the log cabin

Bud and Jo-Anne live in a log cabin with
their children Ben and Sue.

You need 1 cm square dot paper.

Building fences

1 Sue is helping Bud to build a fence to protect the crops.
The garden is a square of side 16 metres.
Make a plan of the garden using a scale of 1 cm to 2 m.

(a) The fence posts have to be 4 metres apart.
How many fence posts will Bud and Sue need?

(b) They want to leave a gap between one pair of
fence posts for a gate. They will nail two 4-metre
planks between all the other fence posts. How
many planks will they need for the fence?

(c) They will make the gates from 4-metre planks.
A plan for the gates is shown. How many 4-metre
planks will they need?

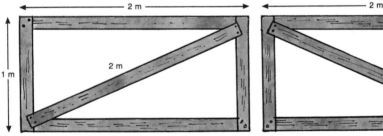

Crop rotation

2 Jo-Anne is using a scale drawing to plan the layout of the garden.
She has divided it into 16 equal squares, as shown below.
She wants to plant fruit (f), beans (b), carrots (c) and potatoes (p).

The plots for each crop
will have the
same shape and area.
Here is the plot for fruit.
Copy the plan.

f		
f	f	f

(a) Design a layout for the garden.
(b) Arrange the crops so that the four centre squares
each contain a different crop.
(c) Design a layout if each plot is T-shaped as shown.

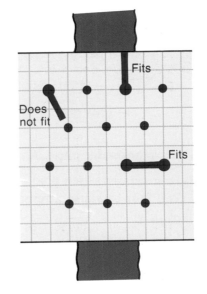

Crossing by raft

3 The family crosses the river on a raft.
The maximum weight the raft can carry is 100 kg.

Bud weighs 75 kg.   Jo-Anne weighs 57 kg.
Ben weighs 46 kg.   Sue weighs 38 kg.

(a) Jo-Anne, Sue and Ben want to cross the river using as few
crossings as possible. In what order should they cross?
Use the model on **Workbook page 15** to record your answer.
(b) What is the least number of crossings needed for the whole
family to cross? Use a similar model to record your answer.

Stepping stones

4 The stepping stones in the river are arranged in a
triangular pattern.

Sue and Ben have a supply of planks.
Each plank will fit between 2 stones in the same row
but will not fit between stones in neighbouring rows.

How can Sue and Ben arrange the planks to cross the
river?
Use the model on **Workbook page 15** to record your
answer.

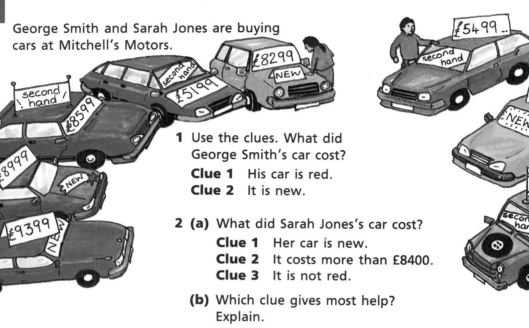

George Smith and Sarah Jones are buying cars at Mitchell's Motors.

1 Use the clues. What did George Smith's car cost?

Clue 1 His car is red.

Clue 2 It is new.

2 (a) What did Sarah Jones's car cost?

Clue 1 Her car is new.

Clue 2 It costs more than £8400.

Clue 3 It is not red.

(b) Which clue gives most help? Explain.

3 Do Workbook page 34, questions 1, 2 and 3.

4 Mitchell's Motors had a raffle. Find the number of the ticket winning second prize. Read all the clues before you start.

Second prize

Clue 1 The number is greater than 50.

Clue 2 It is an odd number.

Clue 3 It is divisible by 5.

Clue 4 It is less than 140.

Clue 5 It is divisible by 9.

5 Mitchell's Motors held a 'Win a Car' competition. Customers had to guess how far the car would travel on 5 litres of petrol. Who won the car?

Clue 1 The number of km is even.

Clue 2 The number of km is greater than 5

Clue 3 The number of m is less than 300.

Clue 4 The number of m is odd.

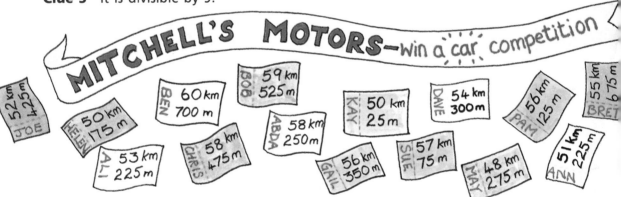

6 Do Workbook page 34, questions 5 and 6.

Challenge

7 Four cars are each made in a different country—Britain, France, Italy and Japan. The four cars are different types and colours.

Clue 1 The French car is red.

Clue 2 The British car is a saloon.

Clue 3 The white car is a hatchback.

Clue 4 The convertible is yellow.

Clue 5 The Japanese car is not white.

Clue 6 The green car is not the estate.

Identify the colour, country and type for each car.

A minibus takes people from the station to the Custom Car Exhibition.

1 These groups of people are at the station waiting to go to the exhibition.

(a) How many people altogether are waiting?

(b) The minibus can seat 12 passengers.
How many trips does the minibus have to make?

(c) Each group wants to stay together on the way to the exhibition.
How many trips must the minibus make now? Explain your answer.

John uses a transporter to bring cars to the exhibition.

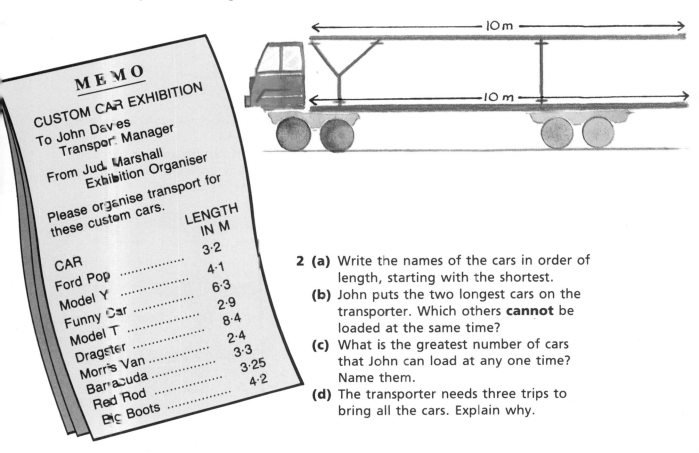

MEMO

CUSTOM CAR EXHIBITION
To John Davies
Transport Manager

From Judi Marshall
Exhibition Organiser

Please organise transport for these custom cars.

CAR	LENGTH IN M
Ford Pop	3·2
Model Y	4·1
Funny Car	6·3
Model T	2·9
Dragster	8·4
Morris Van	2·4
Barracuda	3·3
Red Rod	3·25
Big Boots	4·2

2 (a) Write the names of the cars in order of length, starting with the shortest.

(b) John puts the two longest cars on the transporter. Which others **cannot** be loaded at the same time?

(c) What is the greatest number of cars that John can load at any one time? Name them.

(d) The transporter needs three trips to bring all the cars. Explain why.

1 At Speedwell Sports Ground the
floodlights consist of rows of lamps.
Each lamp can be

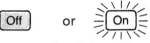

Natasha operates the lights. She can
arrange a row of three lights in **eight**
different ways. Here are two of them:

Draw sketches to show all eight arrangements.

2 Draw sketches to show all the different ways
Natasha can arrange a row of

(a) 1 lamp   **(b)** 2 lamps   **(c)** 4 lamps.

3 Copy and complete this
table:

Number of lamps in a row	1	2	3	4
Number of possible arrangements	2		8	

4 Without drawing, how many different ways can Natasha
arrange a row of **(a)** 5 lamps   **(b)** 10 lamps?
Explain your answers.

5 Here are the entrance gates to
Speedwell.
Each gate can be open or shut.
How many different arrangements of
the gates are possible?

6 Here is a block of eight seats in the
grandstand.
Each seat can be up or down.
How many different arrangements of
the seats are possible?

Challenge

7 For this floodlight, how many different
possible arrangements are there with
four lamps on?

Ask your teacher what to do next.

1 Do Workbook page 35, question 1.

Sandy, the marketing manager of Slimma Soups, wants to find out more about Slimma Soup consumers. She designed a survey to ask 150 men about their favourite Slimma Soups. She drew this pie chart to show the **percentages** of men choosing each soup.

Favourite Slimma Soup
150 men

24% chose tomato soup. To calculate how many men this is find 24% of 150.

Enter **0.24** Press **× 1 5 0 =** to give **36.**

or Enter **150.** Press **× 2 4 %** to give **36.**

The number who chose tomato soup was **36.**

2 How many men chose **(a)** beef **(b)** chicken **(c)** pea **(d)** lentil?

Favourite Slimma Soup
125 women

3 Sandy asked 125 women about their favourite Slimma Soups. Her pie chart shows the **percentages** of women choosing each soup.
How many women chose
(a) tomato **(b)** beef **(c)** chicken
(d) pea **(e)** lentil?

4 You need ½ cm squared paper.

Use your answers to questions 2 and 3.

Sandy wants to present all her information on the same graph.
(a) Copy and complete the graph.
(b) Which is greater – the **number** of men or the **number** of women who chose tomato?
(c) Which is greater – the **percentage** of men or the **percentage** of women who chose tomato?
(d) What do you notice about the lentil soup?

Favourite Slimma Soups

5 Do Workbook page 35, questions 3, 4, 5 and 6.

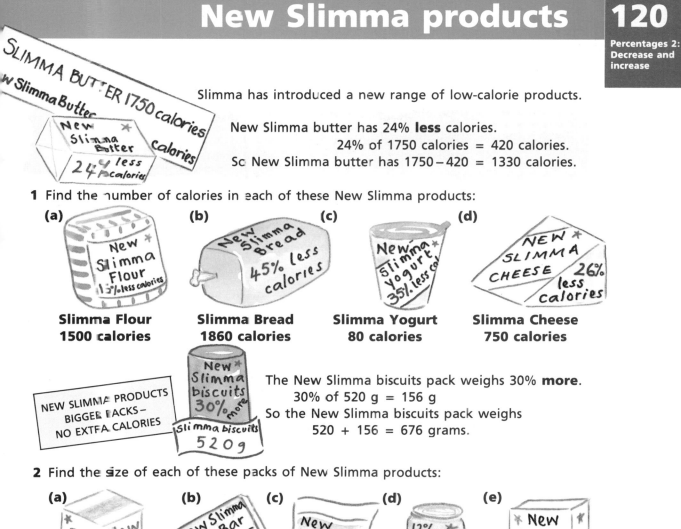

Slimma has introduced a new range of low-calorie products.

New Slimma butter has 24% **less** calories.

24% of 1750 calories = 420 calories.

So New Slimma butter has 1750 − 420 = 1330 calories.

1 Find the number of calories in each of these New Slimma products:

(a) Slimma Flour
1500 calories

(b) Slimma Bread
1860 calories

(c) Slimma Yogurt
80 calories

(d) Slimma Cheese
750 calories

NEW SLIMMA PRODUCTS BIGGER PACKS – NO EXTRA CALORIES

The New Slimma biscuits pack weighs 30% **more**.

30% of 520 g = 156 g

So the New Slimma biscuits pack weighs

520 + 156 = 676 grams.

2 Find the size of each of these packs of New Slimma products:

(a) Slimma Milk
568 ml

(b) Slimma Choc-bar
50 g

(c) Slimma Crisps
120 g

(d) Slimma Juice
300 ml

(e) Slimma Cup-a-Soup
75g

3 (a) The old *Slimma Guide to Eating* has 250 recipes. How many recipes are in the New Slimma Guide?

(b) The New Slimma Guide will normally cost £6·70. As an introductory offer it is priced at a discount of 10%. What is the introductory price?

New Slimma Guide to Eating 18% more recipes

4 The Slimma record *Exercise to Music 1* lasts 36 minutes. How long does *Exercise to Music 2* last?

5 Slimma has changed the prices of some of its sports products. Work out the new prices of the items in the table.

	Old price	Change
Exercise bike	£49·60	20% increase
Exercise rower	£84·50	18% off
Track suit	£37·00	9% more
Training shoes	£23·50	26% less
Swimsuit	£13·80	5% reduction

A group of 150 Supatours holidaymakers
fly to Alicante for a 2-week holiday.

Manuel organises coaches from the
airport to different hotels.

The **fraction** of the group staying at the Hotel Palma is $\frac{36}{150}$.

To find the **percentage** staying at the Hotel Palma,

Enter **36** Press ÷ **1** **5** **0** = to give **0.24**

0·24 is 24 hundredths or 24%.

or Enter **36** Press ÷ **1** **5** **0** % to give **24.**

24% of the group are staying at the Hotel Palma.

1 Here is Manuel's accommodation list. Calculate the
percentage of the Supatours group staying in each hotel.

Supatours Hotels

Palma	36
Nova	
Siesta	48
Paradise	18
Sierra	27
	21
	150

2 Manuel organised these activities. What
percentage of the **whole group** took
part in each activity?

Tennis	24
Golf	51
Bar-B-Q	66
Beach Party	72
Sailing	9

3 There are 120 adults in the group. What percentage of the
group are   **(a)** adults   **(b)** children?

4 Manuel organised a dance for adults only. He sold 84 tickets.
What percentage of the **adults** bought tickets?

5 For the **children** Manuel organised a disco. He sold 18 tickets.
What percentage of the children went to the disco?

Supatours decided to offer more summer holidays. They carried out a survey of 350 adults to find out which type of holiday is most popular.

| Have you had a holiday abroad? | Yes 167 | No 183 |

What percentage of the people interviewed have had a holiday abroad?

Enter **167.** Press **÷ 3 5 0 =** to give **0.4771428**

0·477 142 8 is 0·48 **to the nearest hundredth**.

or Enter **167.** Press **÷ 3 5 0 %** to give **47.714285**

47·714 285 is 48 **to the nearest whole number**.

About **48%** of the people interviewed have been abroad on holiday.

Here are the other questions Supatours asked in the survey. The number of people who chose each answer is given. Calculate, to the nearest whole number, the percentage who gave each answer.

SUPATOURS SURVEY

1 How do you prefer to travel?   Air 251   Rail 32   Road 67

2 What type of accommodation do you prefer?   Hotel 145   Camping 73   Caravan 132

3 Which of these countries would you most like to visit?   France 86   Spain 140   Italy 124

4 Which of these sports would you like to take part in while on holiday?

   Fishing 26   Tennis 106   Sailing 30   Swimming 188

5 Go to Workbook page 36 and show the percentages in questions **1** to **4** in the labelled circles.

6 Look at the percentages in questions **1** to **4**. How could Supatours use these results?

7 Work as a group.
Carry out your own survey about holidays. You may use some of the questions above. Interview as many pupils as possible. Express your results as percentages. Use the circles on **Workbook page 36** to display your results.

Ask your teacher what to do next.

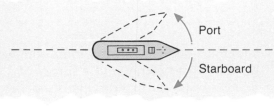

When a ship turns to the **left**
it turns to **port**.

When a ship turns to the **right**
it turns to **starboard**.

1 The *Dragon Duchess* is sailing due West. If it turns
90° to starboard it will be sailing due North.
In what direction would the *Dragon Duchess* be
sailing if it had turned

(a) 90° to port   (b) 180° to port
(c) 180° to starboard   (d) 360°?

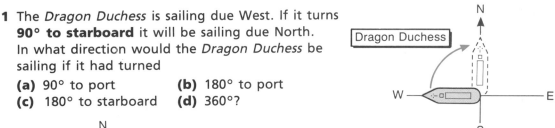

2 The *Queen Bess* is sailing on a bearing of 050°.
In what direction would it be sailing if it turned

(a) 50° to port   (b) 140° to port
(c) 40° to starboard   (d) 130° to starboard
(e) 230° to port   (f) 310° to starboard
(g) 220° to starboard   (h) 320° to port?

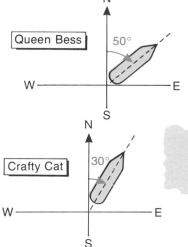

The *Crafty Cat* is sailing on a bearing of 030°.
To change course to due East, the *Crafty Cat* could
turn **either** 60° to starboard **or** 300° to port.

3 In the same way describe **two** possible turns the
Crafty Cat could make to change course to

(a) due North   (b) due South   (c) due West.

4 Here are four more ships sailing on different bearings:

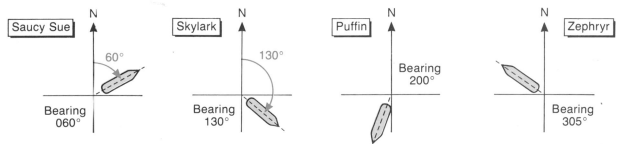

For **each** ship describe the **smallest turn** which would change its course to
(a) due North   (b) due South   (c) due East   (d) due West   (e) a bearing of 100°.

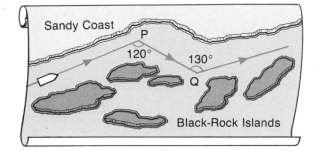

5 The *Saucy Sue*'s navigator plots a
course between Black-Rock Islands and
Sandy Coast.

(a) Describe the turns the *Saucy Sue*
will make at P and Q.

(b) What turns should the *Saucy Sue*
make at Q and P on the return
journey?

Surveyors measure some angles using a theodolite.
They can calculate other angles using the method on this page.

One right angle is 90°.   A straight angle is 180°.   One complete rotation
is 360°.

35°

60°

130°

The red angle is 30°.   The blue angle is 145°.   The green angle is 230°.

1 Calculate the size of each coloured angle.

(a)   **(b)**   **(c)**   **(d)**

50°

62°

120°

45°

(e)   **(f)**   **(g)**   **(h)**   **(i)**

60°

60°

70°   50°

290°

120°

110°

140°

80°

2 (a) Draw two lines, each about 12 cm long, crossing as shown.
Mark the angles p°, q°, r° and s°.
(b) Measure the four marked angles and write their sizes.
(c) Which pairs of angles are equal?
(d) Check what you have found by drawing another
two lines which cross at a different angle.

q°

p°   r°

s°

p and r are called **vertically opposite** angles. q and s are also **vertically opposite.**

3 Calculate the size **in degrees** of each coloured angle.

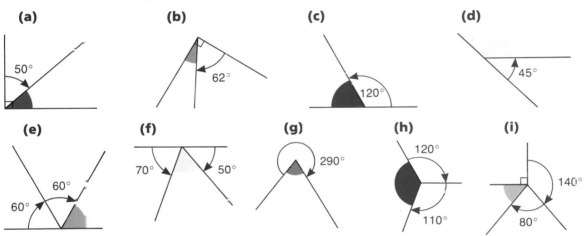

a°

50°

b°

60°   c°

120°

d°

55°   e°

f°

h°

g°   110°

i°

j°   80°

35°   k°

65°

n°   p°

m°   80°

40°   q°

25°   130°

i°   s°   u°

r°

125 Tessellating triangles

**Angles 2:
Sum, of angles
of a triangle**

1 Do Workbook page 37.

2 Here is part of a tessellation of
congruent right-angled triangles.

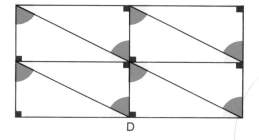

What is the sum of
(a) the three angles at D
(b) the two acute angles at D
(c) the angles of a right-angled triangle?

3 Calculate the size of each of the angles *p* to *v*.

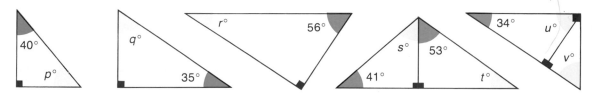

4 Here are parts of tessellations of
• congruent acute-angled triangles   • congruent obtuse-angled triangles.

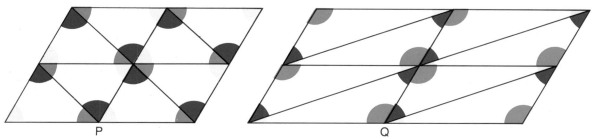

(a) What is the sum of the three coloured angles at • P
                                                        • Q?
(b) What is the sum of the 3 angles of • an acute-angled triangle
                                            • an obtuse-angled triangle?

5 Calculate the size of each angle *a* to *j*.

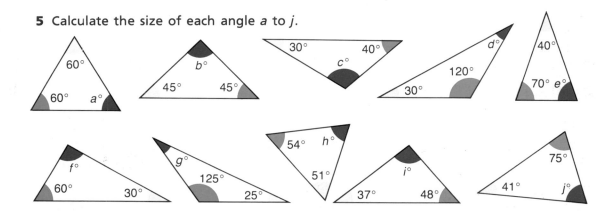

Ask your teacher what to do next.

Gift for young Cousins
£5.79

Gift for older Cousins
£2.49

Gift for Grandmothers
£8.99

Gift for Uncles
£4.39

Gift for Aunts
£2.59

Gift for Friends
£1.25

John is looking at Goodies catalogue for Christmas presents. He is thinking about these items.

1 Write the cost of each item to the **nearest pound**.

> John — Christmas Shopping List
>
> 2 grans .... Fuzz-aways
> 7 friends .... Gift baskets
> 3 young cousins .... Big red phones
> 4 uncles .... Soap-on-a-rope
> 5 aunts .... Luxury soap
> 6 older cousins .... Bath gel

2 Use your answers to question **1** to find
  (a) the approximate cost for each group on John's shopping list
  (b) the approximate total cost of his presents.

3 For the items below:
  • prices under £100 – round to nearest £10
  • prices over £100 – round to nearest £100.
Enter the rounded prices in the table on **Workbook page 38, question 1**.

Shaver
£23.99

Mixer
£27.99

Hair Styler
£12.99

20" Colour Teletext TV Family size set with infra-red remote control; Teletext facility; 20 pre-set channels and electronic search tuning for easy first-time setting up. Complete with matching stand.
£319.99

Food Processor
£64.99

14" Colour Portable TV 10 soft touch buttons
£179.99

Twin Deck HI-FI System Twin cassette deck, Dolby B Noise Reduction, 5-band graphic equaliser, a 3-band stereo tuner and a belt-drive semi-automatic turntable. 30 watts music power per channel.
£239.99

Keyboard
£79.99

VHS Video Get Christmas taped with this fantastic big brand VHS video featuring infra-red remote control, 14 day timer, picture search, pause, frame advance and one touch record.
£429.99

Midi System 50 watts music power per channel.
£359.99

4 Do Workbook page 38.

Floyd and Flora are having a party for 15 of their friends.

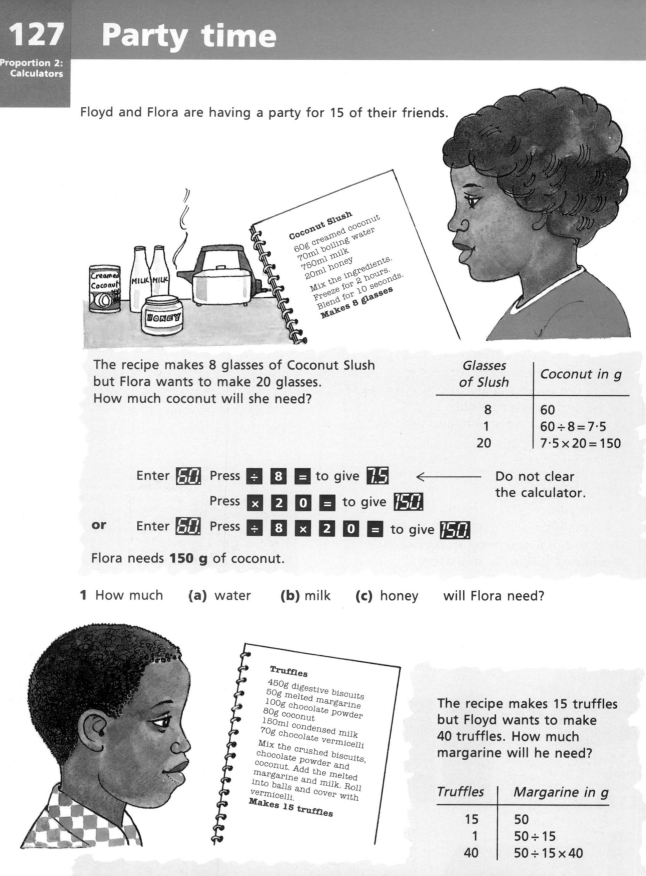

Coconut Slush

60g creamed coconut
70ml boiling water
750ml milk
20ml honey

Mix the ingredients.
Freeze for 2 hours.
Blend for 10 seconds.
Makes 8 glasses

The recipe makes 8 glasses of Coconut Slush
but Flora wants to make 20 glasses.
How much coconut will she need?

Glasses of Slush	Coconut in g
8	60
1	$60 \div 8 = 7 \cdot 5$
20	$7 \cdot 5 \times 20 = 150$

Enter **60** Press **÷** **8** **=** to give **7.5** ← Do not clear the calculator.

Press **×** **2** **0** **=** to give **150**

or Enter **60** Press **÷** **8** **×** **2** **0** **=** to give **150**

Flora needs **150 g** of coconut.

1 How much **(a)** water **(b)** milk **(c)** honey will Flora need?

Truffles

450g digestive biscuits
50g melted margarine
100g chocolate powder
80g coconut
150ml condensed milk
70g chocolate vermicelli

Mix the crushed biscuits,
chocolate powder and
coconut. Add the melted
margarine and milk. Roll
into balls and cover with
vermicelli.
Makes 15 truffles

The recipe makes 15 truffles
but Floyd wants to make
40 truffles. How much
margarine will he need?

Truffles	Margarine in g
15	50
1	$50 \div 15$
40	$50 \div 15 \times 40$

Enter **50** Press **÷** **1** **5** **×** **4** **0** **=** to give **133.33333**

Floyd needs **130 g** of margarine **to the nearest 10 grams**.

2 How much of each ingredient, **to the nearest 10 units**, will Floyd need?

Rock Cakes

225g flour
50g sugar
75g butter
100g sultanas
60ml milk
1 beaten egg

Mix the flour and sugar. Rub in the butter. Stir in the sultanas. Beat in the egg and milk. Place spoonfuls of the mixture on a greased baking tray. Bake for 15 to 20 minutes at Gas Mark 5.
Makes 6 cakes.

3 Floyd wants to make 50 rock cakes.
How much of each ingredient will he need?
Round each answer sensibly.
Discuss your answers with your teacher.

4

Orange Chocolate Milk Shake

275ml fresh orange juice
855ml milk
50g chocolate powder
1 egg

Whisk all the ingredients together. Serve cold.
Makes 6 servings.

Flora wants to make 25 servings of milk shake.
How much of each ingredient should she use?

5

Challenge

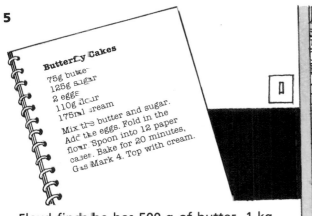

Butterfly Cakes

75g butter
125g sugar
2 eggs
110g flour
175ml cream

Mix the butter and sugar. Add the eggs. Fold in the flour. Spoon into 12 paper cases. Bake for 20 minutes, Gas Mark 4. Top with cream.

Floyd finds he has 500 g of butter, 1 kg of sugar, 1 dozen eggs, 500 g of flour and 1 litre of cream.

What is the maximum number of cakes he can make? Explain your answer.

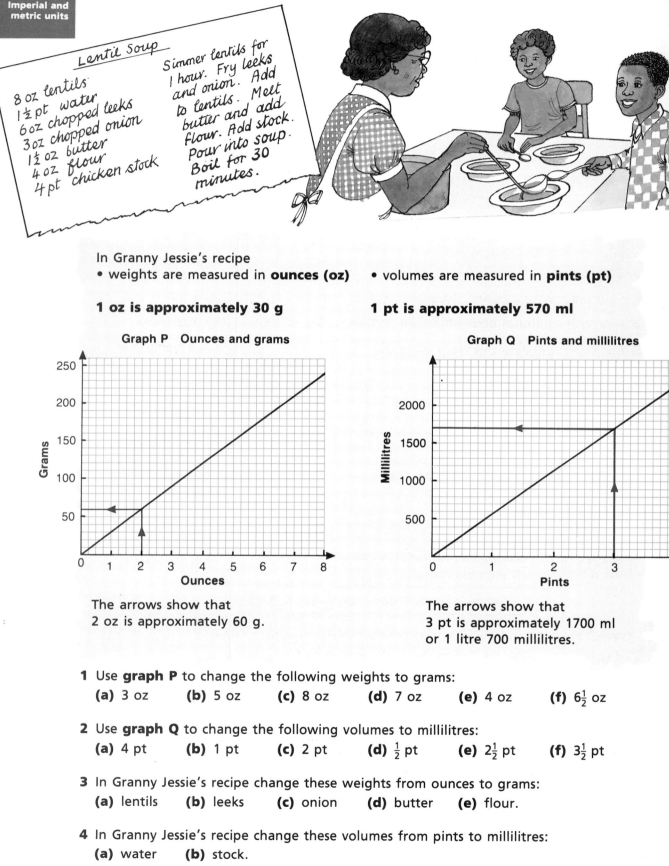

Lentil Soup

8 oz lentils
1½ pt water
6 oz chopped leeks
3 oz chopped onion
1½ oz butter
4 oz flour
4 pt chicken stock

Simmer lentils for 1 hour. Fry leeks and onion. Add to lentils. Melt butter and add flour. Add stock. Pour into soup. Boil for 30 minutes.

In Granny Jessie's recipe
- weights are measured in **ounces (oz)**
- volumes are measured in **pints (pt)**

1 oz is approximately 30 g

1 pt is approximately 570 ml

Graph P Ounces and grams

Graph Q Pints and millilitres

The arrows show that
2 oz is approximately 60 g.

The arrows show that
3 pt is approximately 1700 ml
or 1 litre 700 millilitres.

1 Use **graph P** to change the following weights to grams:

(a) 3 oz   (b) 5 oz   (c) 8 oz   (d) 7 oz   (e) 4 oz   (f) $6\frac{1}{2}$ oz

2 Use **graph Q** to change the following volumes to millilitres:

(a) 4 pt   (b) 1 pt   (c) 2 pt   (d) $\frac{1}{2}$ pt   (e) $2\frac{1}{2}$ pt   (f) $3\frac{1}{2}$ pt

3 In Granny Jessie's recipe change these weights from ounces to grams:

(a) lentils   (b) leeks   (c) onion   (d) butter   (e) flour.

4 In Granny Jessie's recipe change these volumes from pints to millilitres:

(a) water   (b) stock.

5 Write the volume of stock in litres and millilitres.

1 Amir can type 12 complete screen lines in 4 minutes.

(a) Copy and complete this table.

Time in minutes	1	4	8
Number of lines		12	

(b) Use the information in your table to draw
a straight-line graph on squared paper.
Extend the **time** axis to 40 minutes.
Extend the **number of lines** axis to 120.

Use your graph.

2 How many lines can Amir type in **(a)** 20 minutes **(b)** 32 minutes?

3 How many minutes does Amir take to type **(a)** 48 lines **(b)** 102 lines?

4 Copy and complete this table using the
graph of Helen's typing time.

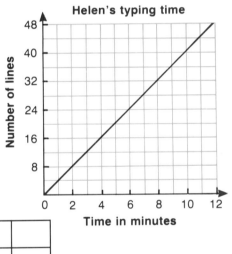

Helen's typing time

Time in minutes	1	2	5	10
Number of lines				

5 What happens to the number of lines
Helen can type when the typing time is

(a) doubled **(b)** multiplied by 5
(c) multiplied by 10?

6 Copy and complete this table using
Helen's graph.

Time in minutes				
Number of lines	48	24	12	8

7 What happens to Helen's typing time when the number of lines is

(a) halved **(b)** divided by 4 **(c)** divided by 6?

When the time increases the number of lines increases **in proportion**.
When the number of lines increases the time increases **in proportion**.

8 Find out how long **you**
would take to type
48 screen lines.

- **You need a computer, a timer,
  squared paper and a book.**
- Do not type for longer than 4 minutes.
- Draw your own **typing time** graph.

9 Forty-eight lines of typing fill one complete page.
Calculate how long you would take to type **(a)** 10 pages **(b)** 100 pages.

10 Repeat question **9** for Amir and for Helen.

Ask your teacher what to do next.

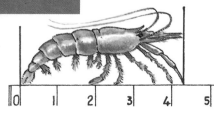

This ruler is marked in **centimetres**. The shrimp is between **4 cm** and **5 cm** long.

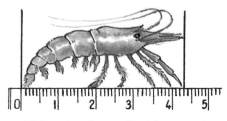

This ruler is marked in **centimetres** and **millimetres**. The shrimp is **4 cm 3 mm** long.

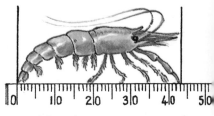

This ruler is marked in **millimetres**. The shrimp is **43 mm** long.

1 Change to **millimetres**: **(a)** 1 cm   **(b)** 3 cm   **(c)** 8 cm 2 mm   **(d)** 15 cm 7 mm.

2 Measure the length, in **millimetres**, of each of these shells.

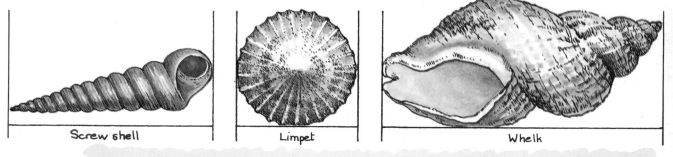

Screw shell   Limpet   Whelk

One millimetre is one tenth of a centimetre. You can write this as 1 mm = 0·1 cm.

3 You can write the length of the screw shell as **54 mm** or **5 cm 4 mm** or **5·4 cm**. Write the lengths of the limpet and whelk in the same way.

4 Measure the widths of the six crabs. Write your answers like this: Pea crab 3·2 cm.

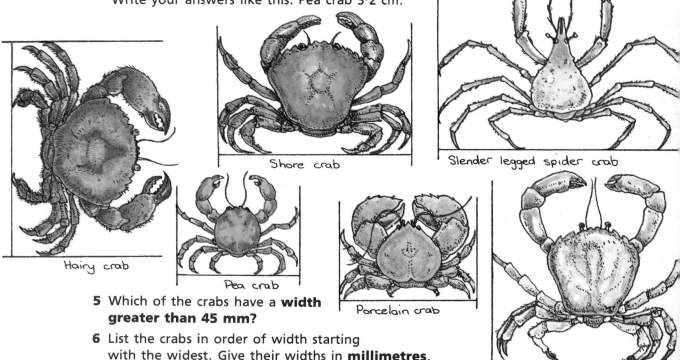

Hairy crab

Shore crab

Slender legged spider crab

Pea crab

Porcelain crab

Pennant's crab

5 Which of the crabs have a **width greater than 45 mm**?

6 List the crabs in order of width starting with the widest. Give their widths in **millimetres**.

This fish is drawn to scale.
Scale **1 cm to 3 cm**.

The fish's true length = $5.3 \times 3 = 15.9$ cm

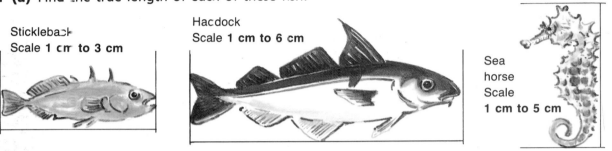

Brown trout

5·3 cm

1 (a) Find the true length of each of these fish.

Stickleback
Scale **1 cm to 3 cm**

Haddock
Scale **1 cm to 6 cm**

Sea horse
Scale
1 cm to 5 cm

(b) List the fish in order of length starting with the shortest.
(c) Give their true lengths in **millimetres**.

2 Find the true length of each of these mammals in   **(a)** centimetres   **(b)** metres.

Common seal
Scale **1 cm to 40 cm**

Dolphin
Scale **1 cm to 60 cm**

Porpoise
Scale **1 cm to 90 cm**

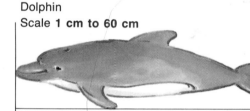

Otter
Scale **1 cm to 15 cm**

Whale
Scale **1 cm to 3 m**

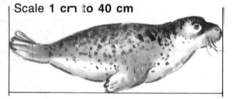

3

Scale   **1 cm represents 5 cm**
means 10 mm represents 50 mm
so   **1 mm represents 5 mm**

Find the true length that 1 mm represents in each drawing in questions **1** and **2**.

4 Some marine biologists are using electronic tags to track dolphins.
Find the true distance of each dolphin from the boat.

Scale 1 cm to 100 m

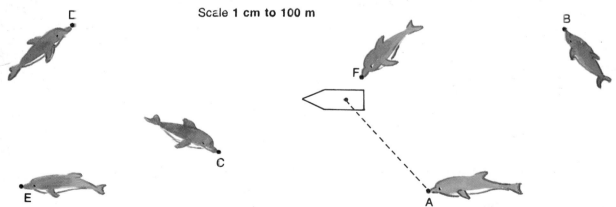

Bronwen's new house

1 Bronwen drew this **scale drawing** of the front of her new house.
The scale is **1 cm to 200 cm**.
You can write this scale as **1:200**.
Each true length is **200 times** the scaled length.

(a) Copy the table below.

(b) Measure the scale drawing and complete your table.

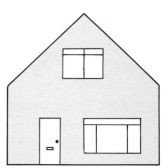

Scale **1:200**

	Length in drawing	True length
Height of house	4 cm	800 cm = 8 m
Width of upstairs window		
Width of door		
Width of downstairs window		
Width of house		

2 This is the ground floor plan of Bronwen's new house.

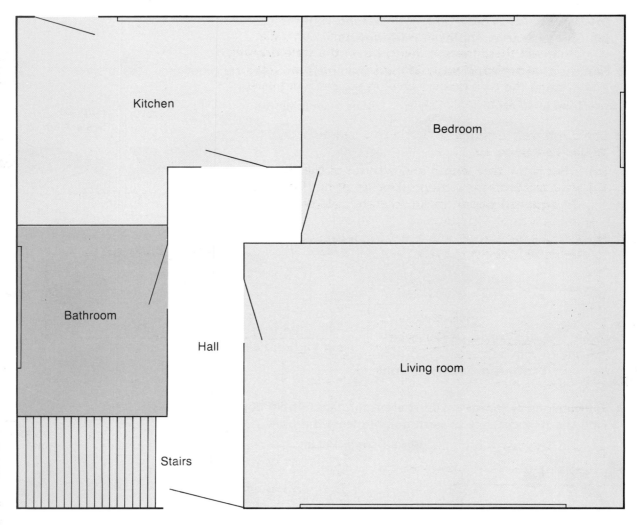

Kitchen

Bedroom

Bathroom

Hall

Living room

Stairs

(a) In the plan the length of the hall is 9 cm. The true length of the hall is 450 cm.
Write the scale of the plan.

(b) Copy and complete this table.

	Length in plan	True length
Hall	9 cm	450 cm = 4 m 50 cm
Living room		
Kitchen		
Bathroom		

1 Bronwen is going to draw a plan of her mum's bedroom
and furniture.
She will use a scale of **1 mm to 20 mm** or **1:20**.

(a) The bedroom is 3600 mm long and 2400 mm wide.
What will these measurements be on the scale drawing?

(b) **Go to Workbook page 28.** Cut out the furniture.
Arrange the furniture sensibly on the bedroom plan.
Stick the furniture in place.

2 There is a scale drawing of Bronwen's bedroom on
Workbook page 29.

(a) What is the true length and breadth of the room?

(b) Here are Bronwen's rough sketches of her furniture.
On squared paper, make accurate scale drawings of
each piece of furniture.

(c) Cut out the furniture and arrange it sensibly in her
bedroom. Stick it in place.

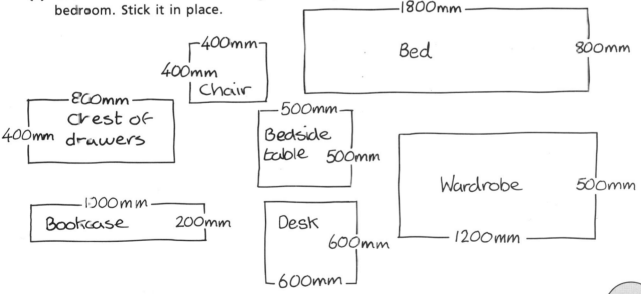

─400mm─
400mm
Chair

─1800mm─
Bed   800mm

─800mm─
Chest of
400mm drawers

─500mm─
Bedside
table 500mm

Wardrobe   500mm

─1200mm─

─1000mm─
Bookcase   200mm

Desk
600mm

─600mm─

3 Make an **accurate scale drawing** of your own bedroom.
Discuss the scale with your teacher.

Challenge

Ask your teacher what to do next.

In 20 seconds Winford ran 100 metres.
In **1 second** he ran 100 ÷ 20 = **5 metres**.
His running speed was **5 metres per second**.

1 Find each speed in **metres per second**.

(a) In 20 seconds
Liz ran 160 m.

(b) Jan cycled 600 m
in 30 seconds.

(c) In 40 seconds
Tony drove 1200 m.

2 Find each speed in **kilometres per hour**.

(a) Barry cycled 72 km
in 3 hours.

(b) The plane took 6 hours
to fly 1236 km.

(c) Azara drove 387 km
in 9 hours.

I've been 3500 m in 6 minutes 51 seconds.

6 minutes 51 seconds is 411 seconds.
In **1 second** Jan cycled 3500 ÷ 411 → `8.515815` metres.
Her cycling speed was about **9 metres per second**.

3 Marion and Duncan are training for a race. Find their running
speeds in **metres per second** to the nearest whole number.
(a) Marion: 1500 m in 3 minutes 58 seconds
(b) Duncan: 17 minutes 2 seconds for 5000 m

4 Find each speed in **kilometres per hour**, to the nearest whole number.

(a) 4000 km in 7 hours

(b) 6 hours for 701 km

(c) 842 km in 9 hours

5 Racing times
Here are some race results.
Find each speed to the nearest whole number.
(a) 100 m in 11 seconds
(b) 49 seconds for 400 m
(c) 40·6 km in 3 hours
(d) 6 hours for 178 km
(e) 10 000 metres in 27 minutes 14 seconds
(f) 3 minutes 50 seconds for 1500 m

The Martin family are on their way back from holiday in France.

Here is a map of their journey home.

The family are travelling by car and ferry from Paris to Manchester.

They plan to travel to Cherbourg at about 70 kilometres per hour.

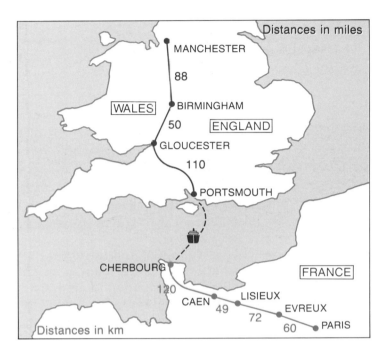

Distances in miles

MANCHESTER
88
BIRMINGHAM
WALES
50   ENGLAND
GLOUCESTER
110
PORTSMOUTH

CHERBOURG
FRANCE
120
LISIEUX
CAEN 49   EVREUX
72
60   PARIS
Distances in km

1 What is the distance, in km, from Paris to Cherbourg?

2 In 1 hour they will travel about 70 km. Copy and complete the table.

Speed 70 km/h	Time	1 hour	2 hours	3 hours	4 hours	5 hours
	Distance	70 km				

3 Between which two towns will they be after driving for **(a)** 2 hours **(b)** 3 hours?

4 About how far will they still be from Cherbourg after **(a)** 3 hours **(b)** 4 hours?

5 They leave Paris at 9 am. Do you think they will catch the 13.00 ferry at Cherbourg? Explain.

6 Repeat questions **2** to **5** for the Macdonalds who planned to travel at 90 km per hour.

7 The Martins plan to leave Portsmouth at 17.30 and travel at a speed of about 50 miles per hour.
In 1 hour they will travel about 50 miles. Copy and complete the table.

Speed 50 mph	Time	1 hour	2 hours	3 hours	4 hours	5 hours
	Distance	50 miles				

8 About how long will they take to reach Gloucester?

9 They plan to take a break in Gloucester and leave at 20.30. Do you think they will reach Manchester by midnight? Explain.

Ask your teacher what to do next.

John Evans does not know how many marbles are in his bag.

His sister Jill gives him 3 more.

John has an **unknown number** + 3 marbles

or **n** + 3 marbles, where **n** is the **unknown number**.

1 (a) Jill has a number of coins. Call this unknown number *n*.
Her father gives her 5 more. How many coins does Jill have now?

(b) John caught a number of fish one morning. Call this unknown number *n*.
He caught 4 fish in the afternoon. How many fish did he catch that day?

(c) The Evans family ate a number of rolls for lunch. Call this unknown number *n*.
They ate six rolls for tea. How many rolls did they eat at the two meals?

(d) Mrs Evans saw 17 birds on the grass and a number of others on the tree.
Call this unknown number *n*. How many birds were there altogether?

(e) A train at the station had 375 passengers. None got off, but a number got on.
Call this unknown number *n*. How many passengers were on the train now?

From the top of the page John has **n + 3** marbles

I now have 17 marbles

So $n + 3 = 17$ This is an **equation**.

$$? + 3 = 17$$
$$14 + 3 = 17$$

$n = 14$ This is the **solution**.

John started with **14** marbles.

2 Use your answers to question **1** and the information below to **make equations** and find their **solutions**.

(a) Jill now has 8 coins. How many did she have to begin with?

(b) John caught 11 fish that day. How many did he catch in the morning?

(c) The family ate fourteen rolls at the two meals. How many did they eat at breakfast?

(d) There were 27 birds in the garden. How many were on the tree?

(e) There were now 425 passengers on the train. How many got on at the station?

3 Find the unknown number in each of these questions.

(a) $n + 9 = 17$	**(b)** $n + 28 = 40$	**(c)** $n + 19 = 38$
(d) $34 + n = 54$	**(e)** $99 + n = 120$	**(f)** $125 + n = 225$
(g) $n + 18 = 46$	**(h)** $50 + n = 102$	**(i)** $n + 13 = 13$
(j) $n + 0 = 39$	**(k)** $240 + n = 542$	**(l)** $n + n = 24$

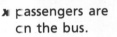

x passengers are on the bus.

12 passengers get off.

20 passengers are left on the bus.

Equation: **x – 12 = 20**

? – 12 = 20
32 – 12 = 20

Solution: **x = 32**   To start with there were **32** passengers on the bus.

1 Use **subtraction** to **make equations** and find their **solutions**.

(a) Jill had *y* tropical fish. Seven fish died. Jill had 12 left.
How many did she have to start with?

(b) John took £*m* on holiday. He spent £29. He had £2 left.
How much money did he take with him?

(c) Mr Evans weighed *w* kilograms. After losing 3 kg he weighed 87 kg.
What was his original weight?

(d) Mrs Evans had a plank of wood *t* centimetres long. She cut off 27 cm.
The length left was 95 cm. What was the total length of the plank?

2 Solve each equation by finding the unknown number.

(a) $y - 7 = 8$ (b) $p - 9 = 10$ (c) $a - 5 = 15$
(d) $x - 15 = 5$ (e) $b - 12 = 32$ (f) $r - 13 = 13$
(g) $w - 27 = 3$ (h) $c - 25 = 4$ (i) $q - 52 = 0$

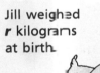

Jill weighed **r** kilograms at birth.

36 kg

She is now **9 times** as heavy.
Equation: **9r = 36**

9 × ? = 36
9 × 4 = 36

Solution: **r = 4**
Jill weighed **4** kilograms at birth.

3 **Make equations** and find their **solutions**.

(a) John has £*u* pocket money. Jill has 3 times as much.
She has £6. How much pocket money does John have?

(b) In the Evans' street there are *n* girls. There are 4 times as many boys.
There are 12 boys. How many girls are there?

(c) Jill walks *h* metres to school. John walks 5 times as far to his school.
John walks 1500 metres to school. How far does Jill walk?

(d) John's last school had *x* pupils. His present school has 6 times as many.
There are 1200 pupils in his present school.
How many were in his last school?

(e) Mrs Evans' part-time typist earns £*a* per week. Mrs Evans earns 8 times as much.
Mrs Evans earns £320 per week. How much does the typist earn?

4 Solve these equations:

(a) $4c = 36$ (b) $2y = 14$ (c) $9p = 63$ (d) $8w = 96$
(e) $7y = 63$ (f) $10s = 130$ (g) $19d = 19$ (h) $5r = 100$
(i) $3e = 39$ (j) $11f = 55$ (k) $6t = 240$ (l) $23q = 0$

I have gro 9 cm since my Tenth birthd

1 In each of the following choose a letter for the unknown number. **Form an equation** and **solve** it.

(a) Some pupils in John's class arranged to go on an outing. Five caught 'flu and could not go. Twenty-seven did go. How many had arranged to go?

(b) Tariq and John are measuring themselves. What was Tariq's height in cm on his tenth birthday?

(c) The Evans kitchen table is rectangular. Its length is 3 times its width. It is 216 cm long. How many centimetres wide is the table?

(d) Six identical weights balance the scales. How many grams is each weight?

(e) Mrs Evans went on a business trip. Her total journey was 305 km. She travelled part of it in the morning. In the afternoon she travelled 175 km. How far did she travel in the morning?

(f) John took ice from the freezer. It weighed 245 g. Some of the ice melted. It then weighed 180 g. What weight of ice melted?

(g) Mr Evans normally works 39 hours per week. Last week he worked some overtime. Altogether he worked 46 hours. How many hours' overtime did he work?

2 Solve these equations.

(a) $t+5=8$
(b) $r-7=3$
(c) $e+12=24$
(d) $2y=16$
(e) $12=w+3$
(f) $16=t-4$
(g) $42=6s$
(h) $9=d-11$
(i) $35+f=50$
(j) $99-a=10$
(k) $81=9m$
(l) $23p=46$

3 For each shape **form an equation** and **solve** it.

(a) t cm, t cm, t cm, t cm
Perimeter = 36 cm

(b) x cm, x cm, x cm
Perimeter = 39 cm

(c) 7 cm, 7 cm, d cm
Perimeter = 17 cm

(d) 5 cm, 12 cm, h cm
Perimeter = 30 cm

(e) l cm, 7 cm
Area = 63 cm²

(f) n cm, n cm
Area = 49 cm²

```
0        1        2        3        4        5        6        7
```

< means 'is less than'.   > means 'is greater than'.
3<5 means '3 is less than 5'.   6>4 means '6 is greater than 4'.

1 Copy each pair of numbers and write < or > between them.
(a) 2   5   **(b)** 7   3   **(c)** 18   11   **(d)** 14   17   **(e)** 27   19   **(f)** 23   61
(g) 2·5   3·1   **(h)** 1·2   5·4   **(i)** 1·6   0·8   **(j)** 4·1   0·9   **(k)** 1·55   1·7   **(l)** 0·4   0·25

⟵ This road sign shows that a driver's speed,
s miles per hour, must be 60 or less.
$s \leqslant 60$ means 's is less than or equal to 60'.

This road sign shows that a driver's speed, ⟶
s miles per hour, must be 30 or more.
$s \geqslant 30$ means 's is greater than or equal to 30'.

$s \leqslant 60$ and $s \geqslant 30$ are called **inequations**.

2 This road sign shows that vehicles
passing under the bridge must have a
height of less than or equal to 14 feet.

Write an inequation using h for the
height in feet of a bus which
(a) can pass under the bridge
(b) cannot pass under the bridge.

3 Write an inequation for the age of each person below.
  (a) Theresa is t years old and is too young to vote.
     Voters must be at least 18 years old.
  (b) You must be at least 17 years old to hold a full driving licence.
     David is d years old and drives to school.

4 From the set of numbers {0, 1, 2, 3, 4, 5, 6, 7, 8, 9}
the numbers greater than or equal to 6 are 6, 7, 8, 9.

The inequation $n \geqslant 6$ has the **solution set** {6, 7, 8, 9}.

         $n < 3$ has the **solution set** {0, 1, 2}

Write the solution set for
(a) $n < 5$ **(b)** $n > 7$ **(c)** $n \leqslant 4$ **(d)** $n \geqslant 5$ **(e)** $n \leqslant 6$ **(f)** $n > 6$.

5 (a) Copy and complete the set of British coins: {1p, 2p, 5p, . . .}
  (b) Terry has six coins of different values. Write the least and
     greatest amounts of money he could have.
  (c) The amount of money Anne has, p pence, is given by $p \geqslant 183$.
     List a possible set of coins that Anne could have.

Ask your teacher what to do next.

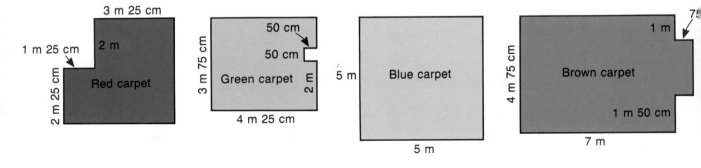

Work as a group.
The Thomson family are moving house.
Billy will get a personal stereo if he
can work out how to cover the floors
of these four rooms with the carpets
from the old house.
The carpets are shown at the bottom
of the page.

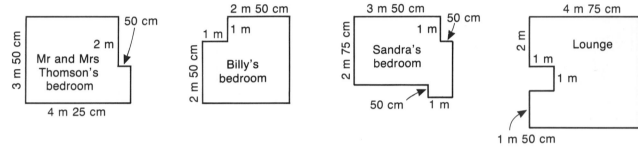

Mr and Mrs Thomson's bedroom — 3 m 50 cm, 50 cm, 2 m, 4 m 25 cm

Billy's bedroom — 2 m 50 cm, 1 m, 1 m, 2 m 50 cm

Sandra's bedroom — 3 m 50 cm, 50 cm, 1 m, 2 m 75 cm, 50 cm, 1 m

Lounge — 4 m 75 cm, 50 cm, 2 m, 1 m, 1 m, 1 m 50 cm

**Mrs Thomson wrote these
instructions to Billy.**

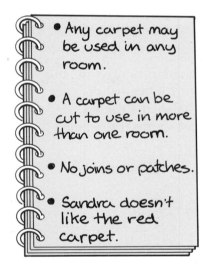

- Any carpet may be used in any room.
- A carpet can be cut to use in more than one room.
- No joins or patches.
- Sandra doesn't like the red carpet.

You need $\frac{1}{2}$ cm squared paper.
Use a scale of **1 cm to 50 cm**.

1 (a) Draw and label a plan of each room.
(b) Cut out each plan.

2 (a) Draw and label a plan of the green carpet.
(b) Cut out the plan. Which rooms will the green
carpet fit?

3 (a) Is it possible for Billy to get his personal stereo?
Explain.
(b) Does Sandra have to have the red carpet? Explain.

Red carpet — 3 m 25 cm, 1 m 25 cm, 2 m, 2 m 25 cm

Green carpet — 50 cm, 50 cm, 3 m 75 cm, 2 m, 4 m 25 cm

Blue carpet — 5 m, 5 m

Brown carpet — 75, 1 m, 4 m 75 cm, 1 m 50 cm, 7 m

Ask your teacher what to do next.

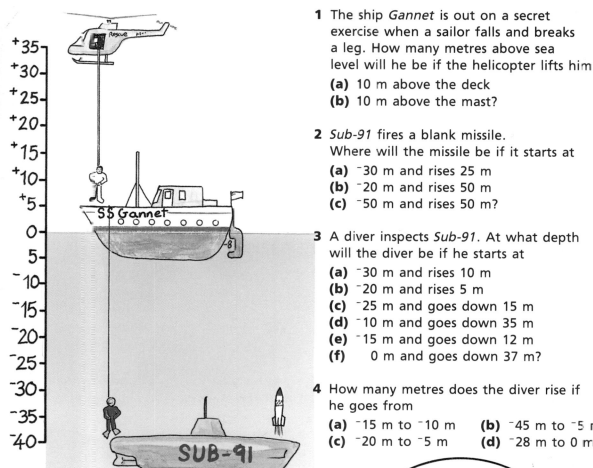

1 The ship *Gannet* is out on a secret exercise when a sailor falls and breaks a leg. How many metres above sea level will he be if the helicopter lifts him

   (a) 10 m above the deck

   (b) 10 m above the mast?

2 *Sub-91* fires a blank missile. Where will the missile be if it starts at

   (a) ⁻30 m and rises 25 m

   (b) ⁻20 m and rises 50 m

   (c) ⁻50 m and rises 50 m?

3 A diver inspects *Sub-91*. At what depth will the diver be if he starts at

   (a) ⁻30 m and rises 10 m

   (b) ⁻20 m and rises 5 m

   (c) ⁻25 m and goes down 15 m

   (d) ⁻10 m and goes down 35 m

   (e) ⁻15 m and goes down 12 m

   (f)   0 m and goes down 37 m?

4 How many metres does the diver rise if he goes from

   (a) ⁻15 m to ⁻10 m   **(b)** ⁻45 m to ⁻5 m

   (c) ⁻20 m to ⁻5 m   **(d)** ⁻28 m to 0 m?

The captain of *Sub-91* sees this ship through his periscope.

The ship is at position ⁻2.

5 Where on the scale would the ship be if it moved

   (a) 5 units to the right

   (b) 9 units to the right

   (c) 4 units to the left?

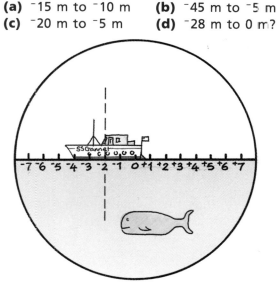

6 Where would the ship be if it started at

   (a) ⁺4 and moved right 1 unit   **(b)** ⁻6 and moved right 6 units

   (c) ⁻4 and moved left 3 units   **(d)** 0 and moved left 15 units?

7 How many units would the ship move if it started at

   (a) ⁺4 and moved to ⁺7   **(b)** ⁻3 and moved to 0

   (c) ⁻1 and moved to ⁺5   **(d)** ⁺5 and moved to ⁻11?

You can write positive numbers without the ⁺ sign. You can write ⁺7 as 7.

You need a die and two counters

1 Play this game with your partner.
Start at zero.
Throw the die in turn.
When you throw an odd number count
up the number track on these pages.
When you throw an even number
count **down**.

First to pass 13 or ⁻13 is the winner.

2 Go to Workbook page 39.

3 On this number line **numbers to the left are smaller than numbers to the right.**

⁻8 ⁻7 ⁻6 ⁻5 ⁻4 ⁻3 ⁻2 ⁻1 0 1 2 3 4 5 6 7 8

Which is smaller?
(a) 4 or 6   **(b)** 3 or ⁻1   **(c)** ⁻4 or 2   **(d)** ⁻5 or ⁻4   **(e)** ⁻26 or ⁻27

3 is less than 6	⁻5 is less than 2	4 is greater than ⁻1	⁻2 is greater than ⁻6
3<6	⁻5<2	4>⁻1	⁻2>⁻6

4 Copy and complete these using the words 'is less than'
or 'is greater than'.
(a) 3 _____ 8   **(b)** 7 _____ 2
(c) 0 _____ 5   **(d)** 4 _____ ⁻7
(e) ⁻2 _____ 6   **(f)** ⁻6 _____ 1

5 Copy each pair of numbers and place < or >
between them.
(a) ⁻5   4   **(b)** 0   ⁻3   **(c)** ⁻2   ⁻8
(d) ⁻70   ⁻60   **(e)** ⁻500   ⁻700   **(f)** ⁻57   ⁻58

6 Arrange the numbers in each set in order, starting
with the smallest.
(a) {10, 1, 4}   **(b)** {8, ⁻1, 2}
(c) {3, ⁻7, 0, 9}   **(d)** {⁻4, ⁻5, 5, 1}
(e) {3, 1, ⁻2, ⁻7}   **(f)** {⁻40, ⁻10, 30, 0}
(g) {⁻20, 0, ⁻80, ⁻50}   **(h)** {⁻30, ⁻5, ⁻100, ⁻1}
(i) {5, ⁻5, ⁻2, 2, 0}

The number strip shows: 0, 1, 2, 3, 4, 5, 6, 7, 8, 9, 10, 11, 12, 13

From the set {⁻5, ⁻4, ⁻3, ⁻2, ⁻1, 0, 1, 2, 3, 4, 5} the numbers greater than 2 are 3, 4, 5.

The **inequation** $n > 2$ has the **solution set** {3, 4, 5}.

You can show the solution set by dots on a number line.

⁻5 ⁻4 ⁻3 ⁻2 ⁻1 0 1 2 3 4 5

7 Do Workbook page 39, question 3.

8

⁻3 + 5 means start at ⁻3 then add 5.	⁻6 + 4 means start at ⁻6 then add 4.
⁻3 + 5 = 2	**⁻6 + 4 = ⁻2**

Find
(a) ⁻3 + 4   (b) ⁻1 + 3   (c) ⁻2 + 5   (d) 0 + 6
(e) ⁻3 + 1   (f) ⁻4 + 2   (g) ⁻7 + 7   (h) ⁻6 + 11

9

3 − 5 means start at 3 then subtract 5.	⁻1 − 2 means start at ⁻1 then subtract 2.
3 − 5 = ⁻2	**⁻1 − 2 = ⁻3**

Find
(a) 3 − 4   (b) 1 − 3   (c) 2 − 5   (d) 0 − 6   (e) ⁻2 − 1
(f) ⁻1 − 3   (g) ⁻2 − 4   (h) ⁻2 − 7   (i) ⁻6 − 1   (j) 8 − 15

You need a red die, a black die and two counters.

10 Play this game with your partner.
Start at zero.
Throw the dice in turn.
Subtract the number on the red die from the number on the black die.
If the answer is a **positive** number, count **up** the number strip.
If the answer is **negative**, count **down**.

First to pass 13 or ⁻13 is the winner.

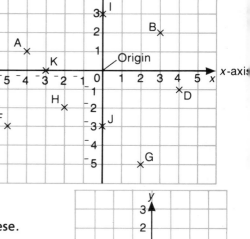

In a coordinate diagram
- the 'horizontal' line is called the **x-axis**
- the 'vertical' line is called the **y-axis**
- the point (0, 0) is called the **origin**.

These axes have been extended to include negative numbers.
Point A has coordinates (⁻4, 1) and can be written A(⁻4, 1).

1 Write the coordinates of the points B to K.

2 Do Workbook page 40, questions 1 and 2.

3 (a) On squared paper draw and label axes like these.
(b) Plot these points:
A(1, 3), B(1,⁻1), C(⁻3,⁻1), D(⁻3, 3)
(c) Join the points in order and join the first and last points. Name the shape.
(d) Draw the diagonals.
(e) Write the coordinates of the point where the diagonals meet.

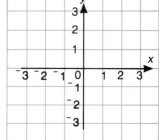

4 Repeat question **3** for these sets of points, using a separate grid for each.
(a) E (1, 2),   F (⁻1, 2),   G (⁻3,⁻2),   H (⁻1,⁻2)
(b) J (⁻1,⁻3),   K (⁻3,⁻1),   L (1, 3),   M (3, 1)
(c) P (2, 1),   Q (3,⁻2),   R (0,⁻3),   S (⁻1, 0)

5 Answer each part of this question on a separate grid.
Plot and join the 3 points in order.
Find the coordinates of a fourth point which completes the shape.
(a)   (⁻3,⁻2),   (0, 0),   (2, 3),   **rhombus**
(b)   (⁻2, 0),   (2, 2),   (⁻1, 2),   **parallelogram**
(c)   (⁻3, 0),   (⁻3, 3),   (0, 3),   **kite**
   Find at least two more kites which have these 3 vertices.

Point A has coordinates (⁻**3, 2**)
- The **x-coordinate** of A is ⁻**3**.
- The **y-coordinate** of A is **2**.

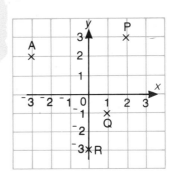

6 Write the x-coordinate of
   (a) P   **(b)** Q   **(c)** R

7 Write the y-coordinate of
   (a) P   **(b)** Q   **(c)** R

8 Do Workbook page 40, questions 3, 4 and 5.

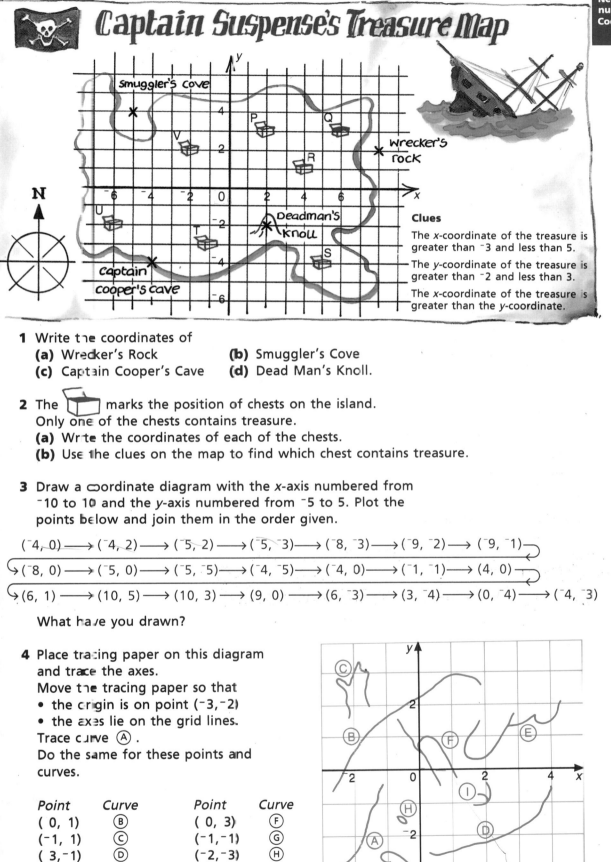

Captain Suspense's Treasure Map

Smuggler's Cove

Wrecker's rock

Deadman's Knoll

Captain cooper's cave

Clues

The x-coordinate of the treasure is greater than ⁻3 and less than 5.

The y-coordinate of the treasure is greater than ⁻2 and less than 3.

The x-coordinate of the treasure is greater than the y-coordinate.

1 Write the coordinates of
(a) Wrecker's Rock (b) Smuggler's Cove
(c) Captain Cooper's Cave (d) Dead Man's Knoll.

2 The ⬚ marks the position of chests on the island.
Only one of the chests contains treasure.
(a) Write the coordinates of each of the chests.
(b) Use the clues on the map to find which chest contains treasure.

3 Draw a coordinate diagram with the x-axis numbered from
⁻10 to 10 and the y-axis numbered from ⁻5 to 5. Plot the
points below and join them in the order given.

(⁻4, 0) ⟶ (⁻4, 2) ⟶ (⁻5, 2) ⟶ (⁻5, ⁻3) ⟶ (⁻8, ⁻3) ⟶ (⁻9, ⁻2) ⟶ (⁻9, ⁻1) ⟶
⟶ (⁻8, 0) ⟶ (⁻5, 0) ⟶ (⁻5, ⁻5) ⟶ (⁻4, ⁻5) ⟶ (⁻4, 0) ⟶ (⁻1, ⁻1) ⟶ (4, 0) ⟶
⟶ (6, 1) ⟶ (10, 5) ⟶ (10, 3) ⟶ (9, 0) ⟶ (6, ⁻3) ⟶ (3, ⁻4) ⟶ (0, ⁻4) ⟶ (⁻4, ⁻3)

What have you drawn?

4 Place tracing paper on this diagram
and trace the axes.
Move the tracing paper so that
• the origin is on point (⁻3,⁻2)
• the axes lie on the grid lines.
Trace curve Ⓐ.
Do the same for these points and
curves.

Point	Curve	Point	Curve
(0, 1)	Ⓑ	(0, 3)	Ⓕ
(⁻1, 1)	Ⓒ	(⁻1,⁻1)	Ⓖ
(3,⁻1)	Ⓓ	(⁻2,⁻3)	Ⓗ
(4, 3)	Ⓔ	(0,⁻2)	Ⓘ

What have you drawn?

Flight to Australia

Planning the holiday

Mary Johnson and her two children, Ricky (10 years) and Jasmine (14 years), live in Glasgow. They plan to visit Australia for a **four-week** holiday.

1 (a) When is the cheapest time to go?
(b) Would this suit the school holidays?

2 In January what would be the cost for
(a) Jasmine **(b)** Ricky **(c)** all three?

3 What would be the total cost for all three if they went in
(a) August **(b)** July?

The Johnsons are planning their Australian tour.

4 What is the cost per person in Australian dollars from
(a) Sydney to Perth
(b) Melbourne to Brisbane?

5 How far is it in kilometres from
(a) Adelaide to Cairns
(b) Darwin to Alice Springs?

Discount return fares		(from Glasgow)
Departures between		
01 Jan – 31 Jan ⎫		
01 Aug – 31 Aug ⎬	£1080	
01 Oct – 9 Dec ⎭		Children under 12 half price
01 Feb – 28 Feb ⎫		
01 July – 31 July ⎬	£1130	
24 Dec – 31 Dec ⎭		
01 Mar – 30 June	£920	
10 Dec – 23 Dec ⎫	£1180	
01 Sept – 30 Sept ⎭		

Cost per person and distance chart

	Alice Springs	Brisbane	Cairns	Darwin	Melbourne	Perth	Sydney
Adelaide	166 / 1320	189 / 1616	265 / 2773	253 / 2623	106 / 650	223 / 2118	153 / 1165
Alice Springs		213 / 2246	178 / 1460	165 / 1307	206 / 1970	214 / 1976	217 / 2021
Brisbane			174 / 1392	268 / 2852	170 / 1379	315 / 3737	116 / 748
Cairns				199 / 1677	259 / 2683	301 / 3436	216 / 1976
Darwin					295 / 3273	269 / 2808	295 / 3328
Melbourne						258 / 2708	112 / 706
Perth							291 / 3278

The yellow square shows the cost from Darwin to Perth is A$269 (Australian dollars) per person and that the distance is 2808 km.

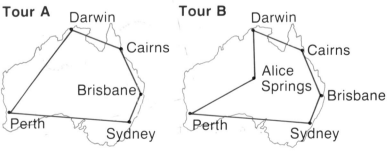

Tour A Darwin, Cairns, Brisbane, Perth, Sydney

Tour B Darwin, Cairns, Alice Springs, Brisbane, Perth, Sydney

6 For each tour find
(a) the total distance the Johnsons would travel
(b) the total cost per person.

7 On which tour could the Johnsons use an Air Pass?

8 For this tour how much would one person save
(a) in dollars **(b)** in pounds, where A$1 = £0·45?

Australian Air Pass
Go anywhere for A$800 per person for up to 10000 km

Planning the flights

Timetable

Depart	Times (days)	Flight number	Type of aircraft	Arrive	Times
Glasgow	0715	BA4853	757	London	0825
"	0815	BA4863	757	"	0925
"	0915	BA4873	757	"	1025
.	and every hour till	.	.	.	.
"	1815	BA4963	757	"	1925
London	1300 (Su, Th)	BA033	L10	Abu Dhabi	1925
"	1530 (W)	BA011	747	"	2155
"	1635 (M)	BA033	L10	"	2300
"	2145 (T, F)	BA011	747	"	0410★
Abu Dhabi	2255 (W)	BA011	747	Singapore	0610★
"	0510 (W, S)	BA011	747	"	1225
Singapore	1325 (M, T, W, F, S)	BA011	747	Sydney	2040

★ means the next day

1 Look at the times and flight numbers for the Glasgow to London flights.
List all the missing times and flight numbers.

2 It takes three hours at London to clear security before boarding the flight to Australia. What is the latest flight the Johnsons could catch from Glasgow to clear customs for the 2145 flight to Abu Dhabi?

3 At what time does the flight leave London for Abu Dhabi on
   (a) Monday   (b) Wednesday   (c) Friday?

4 On what days are there
   (a) flights from Abu Dhabi to Singapore
   (b) no flights from Singapore to Sydney?

5 (a) Which flight would take the shortest time from London to Sydney?
   (b) How long would the Johnsons spend at Abu Dhabi and Singapore if they took this flight?

6 Plan a flight from London that would allow at least a day in Abu Dhabi and at least three days in Singapore.

We will be flying from Glasgow to London to catch the flight to Australia. We stop at Abu Dhabi and Singapore before reaching Sydney.
See you sometime,
love
Jasmine.

Plane spotting

As Jasmine and Ricky wait at Heathrow they spot different types of aircraft. They use a book showing views from the side, the front or below to identify the aircraft.

1 Match each of the aeroplanes above with one of the diagrams below.

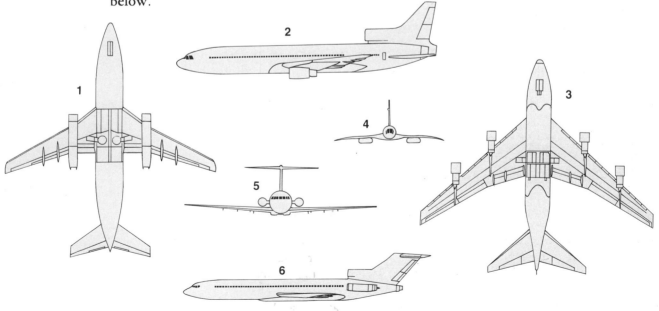

 2 Do Workbook page 41.

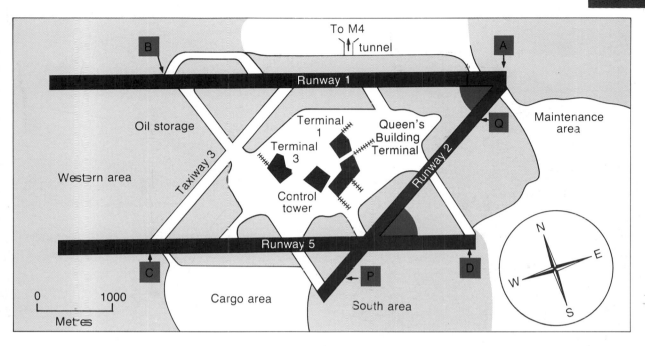

This is a simplified map of Heathrow Airport.

1 The scale on the map shows that 2 cm represents 1000 m.
What does 1 cm represent?

2 (a) Measure the length of Runway 1 from A to B in centimetres.
(b) Calculate the true length from A to B in metres.

3 Find the **full** length of Runway 1 in   **(a)** metres   **(b)** kilometres.

4 A plane starts at A, travels $\frac{2}{3}$ of the full length of Runway 1
and then takes off. What length of runway did it not use?

5 A plane touches down at P on Runway 2 and stops at Q.
What is its landing distance in metres?

6 How far apart, in kilometres, are Runway 1 and Runway 5?

7 Measure the size of the red angle
(a) between Runway 2 and Runway 5
(b) between Runway 2 and Runway 1.

8 Find **both** angles which Taxiway 3 makes with Runway 5.

9 A Jumbo touches down on Runway 5 at C and travels to D.
It turns left to taxi towards the Queen's Building Terminal.
What angle does the nose of the aircraft swing through to make the turn?

10 An A300 Airbus taxies out from Terminal 3 towards B and
turns left on to Runway 1.
What size of angle does it turn through?

Loading and fuelling

Jumbo (with crew)	175 tonnes
Passengers and baggage	65 tonnes maximum
Take-off weight	360 tonnes maximum
Landing weight	260 tonnes maximum

1 (a) Calculate the total weight of a Jumbo with its crew and a maximum load of passengers and baggage.

(b) What weight of fuel can the engineers now load into the Jumbo to give the maximum take-off weight?

(c) What weight of fuel **must** the Jumbo use before it can land?

2 (a) The maximum weight allowed per passenger (including baggage) is 100 kg. What total weight in tonnes is allowed for 410 passengers?

(b) With 410 passengers, what weight of fuel can be loaded to give the maximum take-off weight?

3 Use this diagram to find the maximum weight of fuel the Jumbo's tanks can hold.

4 The engineers pump the fuel into the tanks at 3 tonnes per minute. How long does it take them to pump in 144 tonnes of fuel?

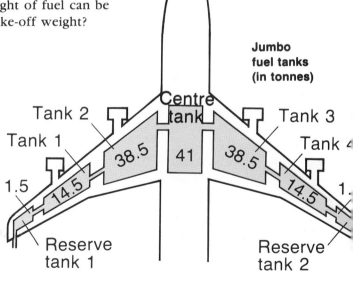

Jumbo fuel tanks (in tonnes)

5 The Jumbo uses 12 tonnes of fuel per hour when flying.

(a) How many hours can it fly on 144 tonnes of fuel?

(b) How much fuel does it use on an 8-hour flight?

(c) On this 8-hour flight the average speed of the Jumbo was 450 mph.
What was the flight distance?

6 In an emergency the Jumbo can jettison fuel in flight at 2 tonnes per minute.
How long would it take to jettison 75 tonnes of fuel?

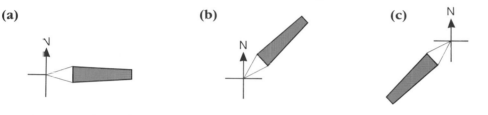

For maximum lift, aircraft should take off and land **into** the wind.

This bird's eye view of a wind sock shows that the wind is blowing **from** the NW.
Aircraft should take off and land in the direction NW.

1 Give the direction **from** which the wind is blowing in each of these.

(a)

(b)

(c)

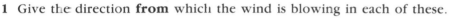

2 Use the map of Heathrow Airport on **Textbook page 150**.
For each wind direction shown in question **1** above, give the runway and the direction in which aircraft should take off and land.

This **side view** of a wind sock shows a very strong or gale force wind.

3 The wind speed gauge (anemometer) on the control tower measures the strength of the wind in mph.
Which of the wind socks below is most likely to show a wind speed of

(a) 5 mph   (b) 10 mph   (c) 25 mph   (d) 40 mph?

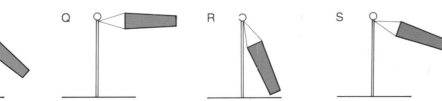

4 When taking off, a fully loaded Jumbo increases its speed by 3 mph every second. How long does it take to reach its lift-off speed of 150 mph?

5 Do **Workbook page 42**.

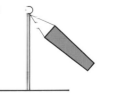

In flight

Ricky   Mrs Johnson   Jasmine

The Johnson family travelled to London in a Trident aircraft.
The picture shows a row of 6 seats and one passage.

1 How many people were disturbed when   **(a)** Ricky left his seat

                                                   (b) Mrs Johnson left her seat

                                                   (c) Jasmine left her seat?

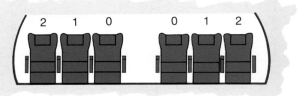

The **disturbance factor** of a row is
the total of all the disturbances.

The **disturbance factor** for this row is
$(2 + 1 + 0) + (0 + 1 + 2) = \mathbf{6}$

2 Calculate the disturbance factor of a row of seats in each of these aircraft.

  (a)   **(b)**   **(c)**

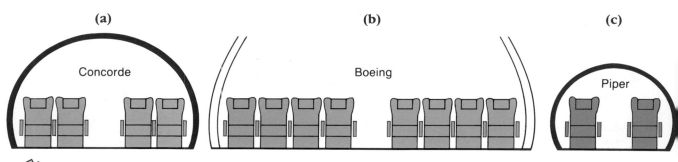

Concorde   Boeing   Piper

3 Do Workbook pages 43 and 44.

4 Japan Airlines have Jumbo Jets which have 11-seat rows.
Use squared paper to investigate the best positions for two passages.

5 An airline is deciding where to put the seats in its aircraft.
What would be the best positions for two passages in a 12-seat row?

Sydney International Airport

This Air Traffic Control radar screen shows aircraft near
Sydney International Airport.

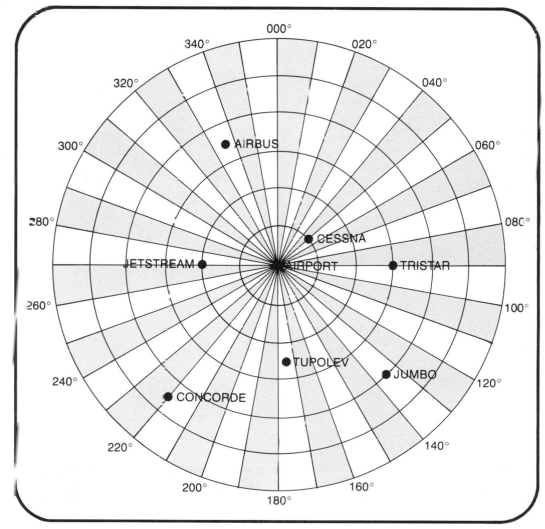

1 Which aircraft is   (a) nearest the airport   (b) furthest from the airport?

2 Which aircraft is on a bearing of 050°?

3 (a) On the screen, how far in centimetres is the Jumbo from the airport?
  (b) The Jumbo is 80 km from the airport. How many kilometres is represented by the
      distance between the circles?

4 Tristar is 60 km from the airport on a bearing of 090°.
  In the same way describe the position of
  (a) Cessna   (b) Jetstream   (c) Jumbo   (d) Concorde   (e) Airbus   (f) Tupolev.

5 Jetstream is due west of the airport. In the same way describe the position of
  (a) Tristar   (b) Jumbo.

6 The Jumbo is approaching the airport into the wind. From which direction is the wind
  blowing?

Touchdown

Sydney Airport

The Jumbo is cleared to land at a height
of 3000 metres.
It descends at 200 metres per minute.
Its height h metres is given by the formula

$h = 3000 - 200t$

where t is the time in minutes.

1 Copy and complete this table.

Time in minutes, t	0	1	2	3	4	5	6	9	12
Height in metres, h	3000				2200				

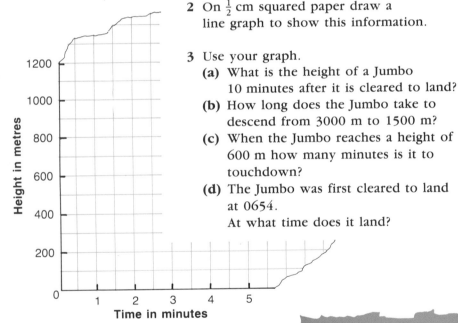

2 On $\frac{1}{2}$ cm squared paper draw a
line graph to show this information.

3 Use your graph.
  (a) What is the height of a Jumbo
      10 minutes after it is cleared to land?
  (b) How long does the Jumbo take to
      descend from 3000 m to 1500 m?
  (c) When the Jumbo reaches a height of
      600 m how many minutes is it to
      touchdown?
  (d) The Jumbo was first cleared to land
      at 0654.
      At what time does it land?

4 Do Workbook page 45.

5 As the Jumbo approached the airport,
Ricky and Jasmine saw Sydney Harbour
Bridge. It is one of the longest steel arch
bridges in the world.
One fifth of its length is over the north
bank, one fifth of its length is over the
south bank and the remaining
303 metres are over the water.
How long is the bridge?

Ask your teacher what to do next.